Praise for Simon's Place

Whether it was President Ronald Reagan, a Portland mayor who drank too much or an obese repeat panhandler, Don DuPay never knew who would be entering Portland's iconic Benson Hotel next. As head of hotel security, the former Portland cop was stunned by the hotel's outdated security policies, and by thefts of bed linen, silver serving trays and even foodstuffs from the chef's kitchen. While attacking multiple security problems, DuPay's duties included interactions with famous musicians, athletes and rock stars – not all of which were pleasant. The clear writing in "*Simon's Place: Stories of the Benson Hotel,*" takes you on a fascinating trip deep inside this historic Portland institution.

~Fred Leeson, author of *Rose City Justice:*
A Legal History of Portland

What I enjoy most about this book and Don DuPay's writing is that he has great skill in bringing you back to a specific time and place in Portland's history. *Simon's Place: Stories of the Benson Hotel* has a great flow that introduces you to interesting characters as it tells the stories of Don's life and the Benson Hotel.

~Bruce Haney, author of *Oregon Moonshine*

Master storyteller Don DuPay takes the reader on a no-holds-barred excursion—from the roof to the basement—of a major hotel—Portland, Oregon's Benson Hotel—in this exquisitely presented piece of reportage. As the head of security for the hundred-year-old temporary home of celebrities, presidents, athletes and the well-to-do, DuPay experiences violence, theft, drugs, alcohol, out-of-control rock musicians and the ash fallout from an erupting volcano. Previously, DuPay has written about his decades-long service as a Portland cop and detective. With the same beautifully-crafted sense of time and environment, the reader follows DuPay's post-police adventures serving and dealing with the guests and staff of one of the major lodgings in the U.S. Not as scary as The Shining but close.

~Robert Crane, author of *My UnHollywood Family*

Don Dupay doesn't just know Portland history—he's lived through it! In these pages, he'll take you on a one-of-a-kind tour of Portland's storied Benson Hotel, replete with intrigue, colorful characters, and enough gritty prose to fill a noir novel. From glamorous guests to the shadowy underbelly of the city, Dupay offers a unique and unforgettable glimpse into the Portland of the past.

~JB Fisher, author of *Echo of Distant Water: The 1958 Disappearance of Portland's Martin Family* and *Portland on the Take* (with JD Chandler)

Simon's Place: Stories of the Benson Hotel, by Don DuPay, is a memorial to the Olde Portland everyone loves to believe they know. People remember a Stumptown of art and creativity going back decades and DuPay does an amazing job of painting that picture, but he also makes sure we see the cracks and the seams. The pages of this book almost turn themselves as we follow the lone security supervisor as he deals with drug dealers, arrogant chefs, aloof celebrities like Bob Dylan, or Ronald Reagan, and immature rock bands, (someone from JOURNEY coldcocked him because DuPay wouldn't let them make sandwiches in the basement kitchen at 4 in the morning). This book is filled with rich histories we should never forget, and it's just a blast to follow in this gum-shoe, Portland pulp narrative.

~Sean Davis, author of *The Wax Bullet War* and
Oregon Wildland Firefighting: A History

Through his signature story-telling style, Dupay—head of security at the Benson Hotel during the last quarter of the previous century—offers a hilarious first-person account of the colorful characters, visiting celebrities, and inside operations inside Portland's most iconic hotel. If you crave historical nonfiction accounts told with wit and wisdom, put this book on your list.

-Suzy Vitello, author of *Faultland and Bitterroot*

Also by Author Don Dupay

Behind the Badge in River City: A Portland Police Memoir—2015

Frank's Revenge: Albina After Dark —2018

The Tainted Rose: Stories of a Portland Detective—2023

Simon's Place

Stories of the Benson Hotel

Simon's Place

Stories of the Benson Hotel

Don DuPay

Oregon Greystone Press
First Edition 2025

Printed in the United States of America

ISBN: 979-8-218-60756-2

First Edition: 2025

This book is a work of nonfiction. Some names have been changed to protect the innocent.

Published by:

Oregon Greystone Press

Phone # (503) 328-9211

tkdupay@gmail.com

https://sites.google.com/site/oregongreystonepress

Interior layout and cover illustration by:
Chris Miller
info@cmiller.com
cmiller.com

Trigger Warning:

There is some violent content.

I dedicate this book to all the people I worked with at the Benson Hotel (and to its current staff), all committed people, for everything they did and continue to do to make the Benson the best luxury hotel in Portland, Oregon!

~Don DuPay

*"No one has the right to die and not leave something
to the public and for the public good."*

~Simon Benson

*"No matter what time of year I come here
[to Portland], people always say the same thing:
'It's not usually like this.'"*

~ Garrison Keillor

*"The power to shape Oregon's future remains where
it has always been — in our collective hands.*

~ Ted Kulongoski

Table of Contents

The First Cup of the Day

It was sometime in 1980, and I was gripping a large beige coffee mug I'd borrowed from the cafeteria as I sat at my desk and ruminated. I was tired and groggy from running around the day before, and tending to the endless tasks of being Director of Security for the elegant Benson Hotel. I was not looking forward to the day ahead of me, because I knew there were many issues that needed tending to at the Benson to make it a genuinely safe hotel.

Massaging my tense neck, I sipped the strong, black coffee, and tried to shake the cobwebs from my mind. What would happen *today* I wondered with a touch of anxiety. I felt exhausted at the day looming ahead of me, as I rested my chin in my left hand, staring vacantly into space. Just as my lids fell closed, I got a call on my portable Motorola Radio.

Here we go, I thought.

The head PBX operator, the voice on the other end of the radio was a sweet elderly lady named Martha or Marty as she preferred to be called. Marty had worked at the Benson Hotel for more years than anyone could remember. "It's been a long time!" she often said with a laugh. "But I like it here. The folks at the Benson are like family. I know most of the regulars and sometimes they call the PBX board just to say hello when they check-in. They like to let me know what room they're staying in, and to hear a familiar voice away from home. So, that's my job!" she said, smiling as she spoke the words to me one sunny afternoon, shortly after I'd been promoted to Director of Security.

Marty usually wore a long, old style 1950s black silk dress, with multiple layers that rustled when she walked. She would pull it up over her knees to get comfortable, as she sat at her "throne" as she called it. With her operator's head-phone set perched atop her gray poodle-do she tirelessly did her job without complaint.

It seemed to me that Marty's spine was a little curved from leaning over the PBX, (private branch exchange) console for so many years, handling all the call routing and multiple inbound and outbound lines. The hotel wags would joke that Marty had been at the Benson so long that it was actually Simon Benson *himself* who had hired her.

The "Lily Waver" Strikes Again

On this shift, I could hear her voice through the radio, a familiar combination of disgust, fatigue and her trademark smirking attitude. "I know you're a little tired and hungover Don, but the lily waver is back again. The lady complaining *this* time is in room 813 and she says he's across the courtyard." I pawed through my top desk drawer looking for the large bottle of Bayer Aspirin I kept stashed there, and swallowed three without water, trying to will my headache away.

"Okay, Marty, I'll get right on it."

"I don't envy you, hon."

Westin hotels were travel partners with *United Airlines* and their regular airline crews. They checked in daily to sleep and relax until their next flight out of PDX. These folks included pilots, copilots, navigators and of course the pretty stewardesses.

One of our regulars, a guy on one of the crews, was frequently exposing himself in front of his courtyard window. He knew the guests in the rooms across from him could see what he was doing and thought he could get away with it. Maybe I would finally catch this misfit in the act. The guy was giving the Benson Hotel a bad name and *that* pissed me off.

The lady in room 813 was *incensed*, Marty warned me.

When I walked up to the room and spoke with the woman, she appeared to be middle-aged; a woman of many years experience. She was not impressed with what she'd seen in the window across the courtyard. I wasn't either when I glanced over her shoulder, and saw the man with his penis in his hand, waving it back and forth and laughing like an idiot. By counting the windows from the corner of the courtyard I could tell "the lily waver" was in room 832, across from 813.

"I'll take care of it Ma'am. I'd pull the blinds if I were you," I suggested. "No sense in giving this nut any more attention." She stood hesitantly, looking down at her pink fluffy slippers, and then turned to go back into her room, but stopped mid-step, turning back to face me: "I thought the Benson Hotel was a *better* place than this!" she said quietly, shaking her head in disappointment.

"I am *so* sorry ma'am!" I said, "Please accept my apologies!" She stood with the door in front of her, and muttered, "I know it's not *your* fault, it's just that...." Her voice trailed off as she closed the door. I knew that room 832 was an "airline" room and that the guy was a pilot. I pulled my radio out of my pocket. "Marty," I asked, "Can you confirm that 832 is occupied by a United Airlines pilot?" After a few moments of silence Marty answered,

"Yes honey…it is a pilot. It's *that* pilot." I smiled grimly putting my radio back in my suit pocket. "Thanks Marty!" I said.

Damn it! The ex-cop in me wanted to go and arrest the bastard immediately, but a criminal case always has to have the victim sign a complaint. In this business, the woman who complained would be checked out the next day and halfway across the country. My satisfaction came only by banging loudly on the guy's door. The man who answered a moment later was now fully dressed in his impressive pilots' uniform with the gold bars on the shoulders, uniforms that many pilots jokingly refer to as their *clown suits*.

"You were wavin' your dick at that lady across the way weren't ya?" I accused him, pointing into the suite and beyond the bright polished window. "She thinks you're disgusting, and I think you should go to jail!" I said, raising my voice and glowering at him.

The pilot made no attempt to defend himself. He just stood there looking surprised with a blank expression on his face, his eyes wide, eyebrows raised, trying to feign dumb innocence. The loose, blank expression on his face told me he was seriously hungover. He realized he'd been caught with his pants down, so to speak, and could offer no excuse.

"Don't ever come back to the Benson!" I yelled. "I'm gonna call the United Airlines office in Seattle and tell HR what you did this morning! We've got all your information, it won't be difficult. And this isn't the *first* time you've been accused of this, either! Pervert!"

I slammed the door in his face, stomped down the hall and took the elevator down to my office on the second floor. After immediately calling United Airlines, I said I needed to lodge a formal complaint about one of their employees, and then I angrily ratted the pilot off. "This is the Benson for Christ's sake! We can't have people like *that* at our hotel!"

I told the man on the other end of the line. "Keep that asshole OUT of my hotel!" I slammed down the telephone receiver, and swallowed two more aspirin. My headache was getting worse, and I still had the whole day ahead of me. As Director of Security at the Benson, I knew it would be eventful.

Interesting Simon Benson Backstory

For those of you who were not raised in the Pacific Northwest, allow me to introduce you to Mr. Simon Benson, builder and owner of the prestigious Benson Hotel. He was a wealthy lumberman, entrepreneur, and a fearless visionary. The Iverson family immigrated to America from Norway in 1868, and wound up working in Wisconsin, in the logging and sawmill industry. For reasons best known to the Iverson family they changed their surname to Benson and later became naturalized U.S. citizens.

After speaking with Simon Benson's great grandson, Chester Benson, also the author of the 2024 book, *Simon Benson: Immigrant, Lumberman, Philanthropist,* I was told about Simon Benson's true name and how naming works in Norway. Chester told me: "Simon's family name is a bit complicated. In Norway at that time they didn't use consistent last names; instead, they

Simon Benson. Photo courtesy of Scott Allen Tice.

used patronymics. You were the son of, or daughter of your father. Simon's father was Berger Iversen, son of Iver. Simon was born Simen Begersen (note the spelling). When the family came to America, Simon and his siblings chose to "Americanize" their names. Simen became Simon, Jon became John, etc. They also decided that Benson was simpler and more American sounding than Bergersen. Almost everyone who writes about Simon Benson gets this wrong. It took a lot of digging to get the correct story."

The dichotomy of this complex man, who was only a teenager when he arrived in America, expressed itself in a myriad of ways and was best demonstrated in the multi-faceted ways in which Simon Benson lived his life. He was a rough and tumble logger, yet he was also a teetotaler who never touched alcohol, while working among heavy-drinking lumberjacks who sometimes looked down on men who didn't drink.

Benson was a laborer with a flair for entrepreneurship and a fondness for the elegance of fine marble and rare, elegant wood, which he favored using in his building practices. Tiring of laboring in the forest, as a humble logger, Benson opened a successful general merchandise store in Black River Falls, Wisconsin. After three years in business a disastrous fire burned his store to the ground, leaving him bankrupt, discouraged and desperate. With a wife and a son to support, Benson, hearing of the emerging logging business in Oregon moved his family to Portland in 1889 and set up shop in Portland.

Benson returned to the lumberjack trade and joined other loggers in Oregon forests, cutting old growth timber with axes and hand-saws and removing the logs with teams of oxen. The entrepreneur in Benson emerged again when he realized there were better ways to remove the cut timber and get it to the sawmills.

Benson introduced the Donkey Steam Engine into his work and replaced oxen with this powerful new method of hauling logs out of the woods. He then began building railroad tracks into the forest to better access the coveted old growth timber, and eventually discovered that "roping logs" together and floating the timber on the nearby Columbia River was a much more expedient way of getting the lumber to the sawmills for quicker cutting and distribution.

Suffice it to say that Simon Benson became quite wealthy in the early years of the 1900s, back when Portland was affectionately dubbed "Stumptown." During this time, Portland was a river community with water access from the Pacific Ocean and was commonly referred to as *River City* by the locals.

An engraved doorknob dating back to the Oregon Hotel

The planning and construction of the hotel was complex. The architects, the leading firm of *Doyle, Patterson & Beach*, began designing the hotel in 1911 in the French Second Empire style, with the Blackstone Hotel in Chicago acting as a design idea. *Doyle, Patterson & Beach* intended to make it one of the leading hotels in the nation, and before it became the Benson Hotel, it was called the Oregon Hotel. Today, some of the supply closets still have the old OH engraved on the doorknobs.

It was an ambitious project for Portland, but after completion in 1913, the hotel subsequently became a lodging for presidents, movie stars, famous musicians and athletes. The new wing opened on March 3rd, 1913, to coincide perfectly with the inauguration of President Woodrow Wilson. This included a telegram sent from Washington for the doors of the Benson to open just as President Wilson began taking the oath of office. It was in 1914 that Simon Benson renamed the new wing, calling it the Hotel Benson.

Dozens of cheap hotels dotted both sides of the Willamette River, dividing Portland east and west of the river. These cheap wooden structures provided housing for timber mill workers and seamen arriving on what people often called "the tall ships." Once set up with a place to rest their heads, the men would look for a brief respite from their labors with the comforts of alcohol and women.

Benson took a dim view of the town's endless alcohol consumption, complaining that a working man, "...couldn't get a drink of water in this town!" He went to some considerable trouble, (after gaining power and influence) to get numerous water fountains installed in the downtown Portland area. He did this by generously donating $10,000 to the city of Portland in 1912 to arrange the purchase and installation of 20 bronze drinking fountains, designed by respected Portland architect, A.E. Doyle.

The fountains became known as "Benson Bubblers." There are two theories why Benson created the water fountains. One, to reduce the rampant alcohol consumption and alcoholism that affected so many Portlanders. The other theory is that it was a small child who inspired Benson to have the fountains created, after he saw a small girl crying at a fourth of July parade, begging her mother for a cold drink of water. In all likelihood, Benson's desire to create the water fountains arose from a combination of both situations. The handsome Benson Bubblers have grown from 20 to 52, and still exist today, providing local Portanders with a drink of cold, clean "sweetwater" as it was called in those long ago times.

Simon Benson with one of his "Benson Bubblers."
Photo courtesy of Scott Allen Tice.

Cheryl Falcone & the Pistol Whipping

I'd been on the job for a couple of months, after first being hired as a security officer in 1979, before I was fast tracked into the position of Director of Security by the former boss. He had found what he considered better employment as Director of Security for the new downtown Marriott, which was set to open in 1980, and he was eager to ditch the Benson.

However, before I was promoted, and still new to the job, the hotel had a bit of drama with a violent assault that ended up making the papers.

On September 9, 1979, while I was making my rounds I heard the distant wail of a woman screaming and in distress. As I was walking along and checking things out, on my regular walk of the floors, I could hear a violent scuffle in the north end of the ninth floor guest corridor. The shouting was coming from outside the door of the luxury suite at Nine North. The ninth floor had something of a reputation for being "haunted" and stories abounded, though I never experienced anything odd while doing my rounds.

That particular suite was regularly occupied by a young gorgeous woman named Cheryl Falcone, aged 35, who worked as the traveling rep of a large cosmetics company. Cheryl was a regular guest at the Benson on her monthly swing through Portland. As she was a regular, she was known by all hotel staff for her flamboyant style and sexy attire. She was rumored to be married but that didn't stop her from flirting with the young bellmen, and any other men who worked at the Benson who happened to be nearby.

I had seen her earlier in the afternoon wiggling her way provocatively across the lobby to the guest elevators. She wore tight black slacks, black business pumps and a thin, ivory, see-through blouse with no bra. The young bellmen twittered as she walked by, but the very proper frontdesk ladies watched her with varying degrees of disapproval and contempt as her pert breasts bounced up and down. I thought she looked like a high-end hooker, but there was no denying it, Cheryl attracted attention wherever she went. With her chin high, a small smile on her face, and her arms swinging, she seemed like the kind of girl who knew how to have a good time.

But not on *that* day. The muffled shouting and yelling became more distinct as I jogged towards Cheryl's room from the far south end of the corridor, still not knowing it was Cheryl being assaulted. "No I didn't!" I heard a woman shout. "Yeah, you did, bitch!" said an angry male voice. "Gimme my money!" the man shouted more than once.

I was growing concerned as I heard the rising panic in the woman's voice, her muffled crying and the unmistakable and ugly sound of metal cracking on a human skull, which instantly brought me back to my days as a street cop working the Albina district in NE Portland.

I rounded the north corner just in time to see that the woman was Cheryl. Her clothes were torn and she was bleeding from more than one laceration on her head. A white man with short gray hair, and of medium height had pushed Cheryl to the floor, as she cowered on her side, trying to shield her face with her arms. The man was about to hit her again on the side of her head with his .45 automatic pistol when he looked up and saw me.

We made eye contact and I glowered at him, a silent threat in my eyes. However, since he had a .45, and I was unarmed that day, (which was unusual for me) I slowly backtracked, retracing my steps around the corner and away from him. Once out of sight, I crouched low to the floor so I would be in a position to up-end him, if he decided to come after me.

Abandoning his assault of Cheryl, he sprinted in my direction, but he turned the corner wide, avoiding me, knowing as he did that I was there. He looked over at me with wide scared eyes for a brief moment, and continued to sprint away. I stood up but remained silent as he took off down the hall, knowing as I did that I couldn't pursue him.

I watched as he scurried to the far end of the corridor and climbed out onto the fire escape, but I couldn't tell if he went up or down the nine floors to the sidewalk below. I stood there for a brief second kicking myself for not having my gun on me, as it might have made a difference. I might have been able to hold him at gunpoint until sworn police officers arrived. The one day I chose not to carry my gun, one of the guests ended up being seriously assaulted.

The irony of it made me angry. *Murphy's Law* always struck when you least expected it.

When the man had run by me I could hear the slide on the automatic pistol rattling, metal on metal, just like the old Colt Army .45 I had carried in 1950s Germany when I served in the Navy during the Cold War. But chasing the guy and tackling him, as much as I desperately wanted to do, was also out of the question. Fighting that natural desire was hard, but I was unarmed at that moment and my *first* obligation was to call paramedics and get Cheryl Falcone to the hospital.

She was bleeding from a cut lower lip as well as the wide gash on her temple, where she'd been pistol whipped, which was beginning to swell and discolor. Her delicate silk blouse was hanging from her waist, in shreds, the fibers twisted and pulled. I helped her up and steadied her as she wiped tears from her face and wiped her perspiring forehead with the back of her hand, catching her breath and leaning into me. "I thought he was gonna kill me," she whispered hoarsely.

By then I had called Marty, the hotel PBX operator on my Motorola Radio. Marty immediately notified Portland Police as well as emergency medics. In only a few minutes, there was a police perimeter set around the entire block hoping to catch the armed man who had committed the brutal assault. More than 20 Portland police officers surrounded the Benson and did a search of all 12 floors which would end up taking almost four hours and running late into the night.

A September 10th article by the *Oregonian Newspaper* read, "Gunman Escapes After Attacking Woman in Benson Hotel." It was also reported that Sgt. John Verhuel, the search team's leader, admitted the search had been unsuccessful. "We didn't locate the suspect," Verhuel told *Oregonian* reporters.

The article got a few pertinent details wrong, but the lead paragraph started out with the usual dramatic flair of the *Oregonian*. "A man who pistol whipped a woman guest of the staid Benson Hotel and held a security officer at bay with a long, silver-barrelled handgun Sunday night eluded a three-hour search of the building by 20 policemen."

The article continues, with a reference to me. "Responding to the alarm, hotel security officer Donald DuPay, a former Portland police detective, arrived on the sixth floor in time to interrupt the assault. However, the attacker threatened DuPay with the gun and made his escape, said Sgt. Dan Noelle, Police Bureau public information officer."

Cheryl Falcone was treated at Holladay Park Hospital for cuts and bruises on her head and the injured hand which she had used to deflect the blows. As the paramedics tended to Cheryl I tried to find out what happened, gently questioning her. "He just followed me off the street and wanted to come into my room!" she explained, with what I recognized as a phony, exaggerated innocence. "When I said no, he hit me on the jaw with his fist and then hit me on the head with that gun he had!" She was emphatic, indignant and looking for sympathy.

"What was the argument *about*?" I pressed, "Something about money?" I suggested meaningfully, looking her in the eyes. "There was no argument!" she said, trying to pretend innocence again. I gazed at her doubtfully, waiting for a better, more logical response. She knew I didn't believe her and that made her angry.

"Come on Cheryl, what *really* happened?" I asked quietly, giving her direct eye contact and the knowing expression that comes from having been a cop and knowing when people lie.

"What are you talking about?!" she snapped. At that point she laughed awkwardly, and looked away, flipping her hair out of her face. As she laid down on the stretcher, and was whisked away, she called after me, aggressively: "He followed me in, and that's *all* that happened!"

Cheryl seemed offended, because she knew I didn't believe her story. It was clear she had been drinking, I could easily see that from her loose way of talking and the smell of booze coming from her. The sweet tinge of alcohol on her breath had been potent.

She also reeked strongly of the department store perfume she always used a bit too generously. She would flamboyantly spray it on her neck and chest, looking around to see if she had an audience as she strutted out the lobby doors onto the sidewalk. With her chin in the air, she behaved as if she was being filmed, like the smiling model-actress Shelly Hack in the *Charlie* Perfume commercials popular in the late 1970s.

Cheryl was a mess, in more ways than one and anyone could see that.

Things were strange from the start, as I would come to find out. Cheryl described the man differently than I remembered, telling police investigators that he had "dark curly hair" when the man's hair had actually been short, straight and salt and pepper gray. Then there was the fact that I knew all too well *why* people give a false description.

After Cheryl was safely in the care of the paramedics, and on her way to the hospital, I located the police commander, who I remember as being Captain Wayne Inman. We spoke and Wayne told me that the suspect had, of course, gotten away. While talking with Captain Inman, I saw the crowd of police gathered in front of the Benson, as well as several newspaper photographers milling about. This was disconcerting and exactly the kind of attention a downtown luxury hotel like the Benson *didn't* need.

To make matters worse, there was an even larger crowd of curious spectators gathering from the Artquake festival which was happening on SW Sixth one block away. *The Oregonian* described the situation accurately and amusingly:

"Police had their hands full keeping spectators from swarming over from Broadway, where blinking lights on patrol cars advertised the activity.

Art Quake officials, in cooperation with police, sought and received from the Oregon Liquor Commision, emergency authority to keep a cabaret open beyond its scheduled time in the basement of the Meier & Frank department store's parking garage.

The festival's permit to serve beer there expired at 8 p.m., but with OLCC approval continued serving until 9:30 p.m. Officials also convinced a musical group that was playing, Upepo, to stay on for an hour and 45 minutes past its scheduled 7:30 departure time.

Those measures helped keep the Art Quake crowd occupied in the cabaret, instead of gathering near the Benson, said Art Quake staff member Marta Melinger. She estimated that 500 to 1,000 persons joined 1,000 already in the cabaret when the band and beer extensions were arranged. As a further inducement to keep people off the streets, Art Quake officials discontinued the cabaret's $1 cover charge."

There was a party vibe in the street as the police conducted their search. People stood across the street, drunk, pointing and laughing. What a day for this to occur, on the same day as the Art Quake festival!

During the commotion of the search, which took four hours, until well past 10:00 p.m., kitchen staff provided free coffee and sandwiches for all those guests and visitors who were stuck in the main lobby. They could not go back to their rooms after being evacuated, but could also not leave the hotel. Just as the search ended, staff had begun handing out bedding, like blankets and pillows to those stuck in the lobby.

It was an embarrassing and chaotic night and we were all relieved when the search was called off, after it became obvious the gunman had gotten away long ago. The man never was found, but I'd done my job, providing "reasonable care" to Cheryl Falcone. By the grace of God, I was the first on the scene, prevented a more serious assault from occurring by an armed man, obtained immediate medical care for Cheryl Falcone, and arranged for police and an ambulance to come right away.

Still, I could smell the stench of a lawsuit looming on the horizon.

The more I thought about it, the less likely I thought Cheryl had been followed off the street. My experience as a police officer and later as a Detective with the Portland Police Bureau told me something else entirely. It smelled more like a dope deal gone bad, and that was exactly what I suggested to the cops as well as my bosses at the hotel, later, when I spoke with them about it.

Working for the Benson might be more dangerous than I anticipated, but I also knew the attack was a random and rare event. As a former street cop, I had faced gunmen before but it was a long time since that had happened. The assault caught me by surprise and made me rethink not carrying a gun while on duty at the Benson. I knew danger was just around the corner, and could present itself unexpectedly, as in this case, but I also knew what had likely happened between the colorful Cheryl Falcone and the man she claimed just "followed" her into the hotel was *not* as simple as she insisted.

The hotel General Manager, Paul Mannerly, (son of renowned hotel entrepreneur Lynn Himmelman) was justifiably concerned about a potential lawsuit. As I stood in his office, I assured him that we had acted in exactly the correct manner. And that Cheryl Falcone winning a negligence lawsuit against the Benson was highly unlikely, particularly if I testified about what I had witnessed, *and* overheard when the man was assaulting her.

No Key Control Meant No Guest Safety

Previously while working as a Portland police officer, the district attorney kept us apprised of new case law that might dictate our actions. This included such things as the famous Miranda Warning, which began in June of 1966, five years after I'd become a sworn officer, and how *that* changed law enforcement forever.

When I first took the job at the Benson, a few days after I'd been hired, I went to the Central Library and did research on case law defining the obligations of the hotel industry. I realized I needed to beef up my knowledge of what constituted *current* case law and what we at the Benson could expect. To facilitate that process, I also subscribed to a monthly printed newsletter that described various lawsuits against hotels and what the courts had determined to be "reasonable care," for guests.

Most everyone working in hotel security knew the sad story of the popular singer Connie Francis and what happened to her. While traveling, Francis had been brutally raped in a New York Howard Johnson Motel room November 8th of 1974. The industry buzz about her case, (and what I related to Mannerly about the case) gave my insight into hotel security *and* my concerns some serious credibility.

In the Connie Francis case, "reasonable care" had been tossed out the window and the NY motel paid through the nose when she was awarded 2.5 million dollars in a later settlement, all of which she deserved. The motel had failed to keep her safe, and she spent decades struggling to recover from the trauma of being raped at knifepoint and terrorized for almost three hours by an assailant and robber who was never caught.

I recall after almost four months on the job as a *security officer* I was promoted to Director of Security. It was not long after being promoted that one afternoon while I was drinking hot coffee and eating a delicious pastrami sandwich, that I had an unwelcome epiphany! The hotel had so many potential legal issues because of lax security, that I realized it was not safe for *anyone* to stay at the famously elegant Benson Hotel, not even *me.*

For instance hotel management had no concept or understanding of what guest room "key control" was and *why* it was important. They had no idea how many room keys had been issued to guests and never returned over the intervening years. This is priority number one for hotel security, for *any* hotel, and particularly at that time in the early 1980s. I remember asking the maintenance engineer, a grey-haired man in his 50s named Frank, how many sets of Benson Hotel keys were floating around Portland. He looked at me quizzically, and admitted he didn't know.

"Hundreds, I reckon. The rooms have never been rekeyed, you know."

"What?"

"Well, yeah. The rooms haven't been rekeyed, not since the hotel opened in 1913, I guess?"

I was flabbergasted. I couldn't believe it. At first I thought he was joking, but Frank was a nice guy, hardworking and honest. He fixed everything that went wrong at the Benson. Toilets, sinks, the stoves and ovens in the kitchen and maintained the basement boiler room, which provided hot water, and heat for the entire building. The steam heating boilers were lovingly maintained by Frank, who took real pride in his work. I could tell by his surprised and blank expression that he was being completely honest when he admitted the rooms had never been rekeyed. But I was still stunned. If there were hundreds of keys just floating around Portland and had been for decades, that meant not *one* guest was safe staying at the Benson.

If I stayed in *any* room, the door could easily be opened by any number of former guests who might have stayed there and kept the key as a souvenir. The thought struck terror in my jaded heart, thinking of the potential danger to guests and the likelihood of a possible lawsuit because of an assault or worse yet, a rape. That was *all* the Benson needed — a lawsuit. The only real way to be truly safe in one of the rooms was to push the heavy dresser in front of the door at bedtime and hope for the best. The other serious issue was that there was not one person to respond in case of a fire, in other words, there was no trained *Emergency Response Team.*

When Frank told me the abysmal truth about key control, or lack thereof, I told him I would be handling cutting all future keys and that we would begin the long, time consuming process of finally rekeying every single room. Frank was delighted to hand over that tedious responsibility to me as it freed him up to do more of what he was supposed to be doing in the basement boiler room.

Most shocking of all was that there was not a single *smoke detector* in the entire building! Not *one* smoke detector in any one of the guest rooms and not one smoke detector in the corridors or basement halls. Again, when I found this out, as told to me by Frank, I was stunned.

The Benson Hotel was a Disaster

Because the Benson had opened for business in 1913 as an annex to the adjacent Oregon Hotel next door, I knew the building had no sprinkler system. Pray you could remember where the fire escape was located if the place ever caught fire one lonely night in the middle of a dry summer. The hotel was a ticking time-bomb and that worried me.

To make the situation worse, the fire marshal explained to me one afternoon, (after I called him to come over and discuss safety issues) that because of the large fussy canopy overhanging the Broadway street entrance, their big truck with the imposing fire ladder wouldn't be able to get close enough to the building to rescue anyone higher up than the fifth floor, unless it was unceremoniously torn off and that would take precious time. Even if the canopy was removed the ladder would *still* not be able to get higher than the fifth floor, he told me.

Pragmatically, in case of an emergency of any kind, especially above the fifth floor, the hotel guests would be on their own. I had to fix these problems, but it would take time and a lot of money, and some of these problems might require *threats* to solve.

I could see that the old and accepted ways of doing business *and* maintenance at the Benson Hotel were going to be hard to change. The Benson management team was living in a bygone era, a dreamworld. They were still operating from the days when hotel security was personified by a middle-aged hotel detective sitting in the lobby pretending to read the newspaper, glancing over the top when a suspected prostitute walked by with a wiggle in her step and a come hither glance.

Maybe that old detective would help if he could when the fire department rushed in and tried to rescue everybody at the first sign of smoke, but he wouldn't be able to do much. This was the environment I found myself in when I took the job of Director of Security. However, I was not just the new "security guy," as I was sometimes referred to, I was a modern and professional "risk manager," with nearly twenty years experience in police work. This included over ten years I spent working as a burglary detective, which helped inform my understanding of risk management and the law of averages.

The main challenge would be the mountain of opposition I would have to overcome.

I always did my best, every day, but I understood the dinosaurs would have to be rooted out and the old dragon's slayed before any improvements could be made. But I was determined to do what I knew needed to be done. Not only did I worry about the safety of guests, but I worried about the fate of the actual building.

I had numerous meetings with the General Manager of the hotel, Paul Mannerly, about these ongoing and potentially dangerous issues. I was able to use the leverage of the notorious 1974 Connie Francis lawsuit to impress upon Paul the importance of this new reality regarding "hotel liability" and hopefully steer his thinking in a new, safer direction for all concerned.

Paul was, after all, responsible for this iconic but dangerously outdated monument to opulence known as the Benson Hotel. He was, as mentioned previously, the son of Lynn Himmelman, who was a true empire builder in the hospitality industry, much like Simon Benson himself had been. Himmelman created Western Hotels, which became Western International Hotels and then later became known as Westin Hotels.

Westin Hotels managed some of the premier properties around the country including the Ilikai Hotel in Honolulu, the Westin Bonaventure in Los Angeles, and The Plaza Hotel in New York City overlooking Central Park. Westin was big league and the Benson remained one of the oldest and best hotels in Portland. I had heard that Daddy Himmelman had arranged for his son Paul to attend Cornell University's hospitality school, but Paul didn't seem to have his father's business sense or innate ability to lead in quite the same way Lynn Himmelman was famous for having.

Paul often floundered in his responsibilities and when I had to visit him in his office, to discuss some problem or concern, (like the complete lack of smoke detectors) I repeatedly watched him nervously arrange and rearrange the papers on his desk, in an attempt to make me think he was doing something productive. Paul knew, for example, that when I wanted to talk with him, he would be put in a position of some discomfort for the simple reason that he'd have to make some hard decisions about safety and that meant money and justifying the expense of upgrades to his father, whom I had heard could be quite stern. In the end, Lynn Himmelman must have understood the reasoning behind my demands that the Benson be upgraded, because the upgrades did eventually take place.

"How much are all those smoke detectors going to cost and how about batteries for them? And how can we afford to rekey ALL of these guest rooms?" Paul asked me one afternoon. My answer was always the same, "The Benson can't afford *not* to. It's as simple as that. Do you want this old hotel to go up in a cloud of smoke? Kitchen fires happen all the time."

I often felt sorry for Paul because besides my regular haranguing of him, he was also at the mercy of the renowned Executive Chef. Xavier Bauser was the man who stormed around the Benson like a veritable God, clacking around in his Dutchboy Wooden clogs and furiously barking orders at those who worked under him. Paul's father must have told him not to do *anything* to upset *The God of Food* sent down to earth to grace the Benson Hotel for it was clear Paul was intimidated by Chef Bauser.

But then so was everyone else at the Benson!

When the Benson first opened, Simon Benson originally hired the renowned chef Henry Thiele, of the famously popular Henry Thiele Restaurant, which was located near NW 23rd Avenue. Thiele was hired as the "chief steward" and set the standard for excellent cuisine at the Benson thereafter. As a result of his large menu and personable rapport with customers, Henry Thiele helped make the Benson a social and culinary success. Chef Bauser, (who was equal to Thiele in his culinary expertise) was treated with a great deal of deference and was allowed to get away with a lot even despite his volatile management style.

Bauser intimidated the employees regularly.

Except *me*.

I had been a street cop in the rough Albina district, and a police detective for over eleven years, before health issues compelled me to resign from PPB. I resigned because my personal physician told me the stress of police work would "kill" me "in the end." In all that time with the police, I learned a lot, like most cops do regarding the human condition and about people. I saw Bauser in a realistic light, and was not intimidated by him.

The Superstar Chef
& the Purchasing Agent

Not much scared me, particularly not a chubby little cook with a big ego and loud wooden clogs who stormed about barking orders about how to prepare *food* to his intimidated underlings. But to his credit, Swiss born Xavier Bauser was a true '*Arteest*' at what he did. He provided the exquisite cuisine that was the hallmark of the famous London Grill Restaurant. He provided world-class food for the almost daily banquets for as many as three hundred of Portland's power elite. Bauser oversaw all the room service food that was ordered for the *famous* guests who stayed at the Benson and made certain it was correctly served on silver trays by formally dressed room service waiters, with perfect manners, good verbal skills and a formal and erudite manner.

In short, Bauser was a superman who somehow survived the unbelievable daily stress of his profession, and he did so in his apparently comfortable but ridiculous looking wooden clad feet. But as good as he was at his profession, Bauser was also a serious liability to the hotel in other ways. The sad truth is that Bauser could be a caustic, sarcastic, nasty-mouthed, little bastard who terrified the women who had to work around him. This included dozens of banquet and cocktail servers, and any other generally polite, friendly female employees who happened to cross his path when he was in one of his "moods" which could occur at any time and for no apparent reason.

One afternoon I sat eating lunch in the employee cafeteria with the Hotel Purchasing Agent. Janet was a friendly, even tempered, dark-haired woman with a quick wit who generally liked everyone. She was almost always in a great mood. But not that day. She was chewing her food furiously, obviously angry about something. After some gentle prodding on my part, she shared with me that she was *extremely* tired of both listening to and being a victim of Bauser's nasty tirades. This included when something the chef had ordered through her purchasing office hadn't, "arrived on time" or was not up to his exact specifications.

In a voice loud enough to be overheard by others, she said: "If he opens up his filthy mouth at me one more time, I'm going to knock him flat. I may lose my job but he'll lose some teeth!" I smiled at her vehemence and continued to calmly eat my salad.

"Come on now, Janet. Let me talk to Xavier. I'll work it out."

As Janet furiously chewed her food, I noticed that several other employees eating their lunch nearby were looking down, staring at their food in embarrassment but listening intently to our conversation. One or two twittered, looked up and chuckled, but not one person defended or stood up for the chef. Then I saw they began glancing over periodically at the cafeteria door. It was clear they were worried that the notorious Bauser might storm through at any time, walk over to them, and fly into one of his infamous and inexplicable rages, perhaps over the questionable quality of some limp cucumbers, or because the kitchen floor was sticky from spilled sugar.

The Hotel Benson Grille, 1910. Photo courtesy of Scott Allen Tice.

I could see Bauser's regular verbal abuse was becoming a serious problem. He was coming close to eliciting physical violence among the female employees, and in this case, a very nice lady named Janet. How would that look on the local evening news, I wondered to myself. I envisioned a headline that read something like… *Benson Hotel Purchasing Agent punches Executive Chef Xaiver Bauser, and Breaks his Nose in Fight over Cake Flour Arriving Late*. I smiled as I continued to eat my salad, thinking of the next chore I'd have to take on while trying to keep the peace among the employees.

Another Lecture From Yours Truly

I could see it was time to give Paul Mannerly another one of my "risk management" lectures that I knew he dreaded. I'm sure that to him I was just another detail obsessed former cop who had handed over his police badge for another badge - that of the Director of Security but that I had remained at heart yet another tedious *rule crazy cop*.

After lunch, one afternoon, I knocked on Paul's private office door. Left partially ajar, I could hear his toilet flushing before he called for me to come in. His beautiful walnut paneled office, with its formal mahogany executive desk and plush burgundy carpeting had a private restroom. I guess he deemed it inappropriate to pee with the rest of the boys in the adjacent mezzanine level, sparkling clean, public restroom that we were all happy to use, but I couldn't blame him. If I had the option of a private restroom, I'd have been happy as well.

As I entered his office, he immediately began shuffling papers on his desk. His body language told me he was busy and hoped

I wouldn't take long. I hit him right between the eyes with it. "Paul, Chef Bauser is being verbally abusive to some of the female employees." He sighed and as I recall whispered under his breath: "Oh, Jesus, not again."

"I'm sorry, but it's true. It's deteriorated to the point that one of the ladies is ready to punch his lights out. You know Janet?" He nodded his head.

At this point, I stopped speaking and smiled slowly, chuckling, savoring the moment, seeing the comedy of it for the first time. "Something has to be done before you wind up on the short end of a discrimination lawsuit. I'm sure you're aware of his nasty mouth. I've heard it myself. The men can take it, but the women are more sensitive. They're about to sue *or* fight him in the kitchen with their fists."

"I know," Paul admitted, standing up now and pacing back and forth behind his desk. "But he's so hard to talk to… he's just…" His voice trailed off and his face was furrowed with concern. It was clear this was a stinker of a situation Paul wanted nothing to do with.

"I'll talk to him if you want me to?" I volunteered with hopeful relish. Paul knew I meant it, too. "No, no! I'll have to speak to him. I'll talk to him about his conduct, myself. I can take care of this!" he promised. I routinely felt sorry for Paul. Though he was taller than my six feet, he was habitually unhappy looking. He was generally youthful looking, with a pleasant face, but his thinning hair made him appear older than a man in his middle thirties and I suspected there was a part of him that resented me. I was almost fifteen years older, and had far more life and work experience. I know there must have been times when he felt his lot in life as the manager of the Benson Hotel seemed unfair.

I also knew that Paul was at the very least intimidated by Bauser, but forced into the position of having to do something about him. The shadow of his father must have loomed over his head and I knew Paul definitely did *not* want the hotel sued. During the next few weeks, after my conversation with Paul and *his* conversation with the Chef, Bauser seemed to be on his best behavior.

From that moment on, he and the purchasing agent, Janet, merely glared at each other and spoke woodenly and only when absolutely necessary. The Chef turned in his purchase orders to her in-box, (she was clearly his Nemesis) and *he* avoided her. I hoped my intervention had once again saved us a lawsuit. Or a fist fight.

Writing New Policy to Ensure Hotel Safety

In my spare time I read over the Benson Hotel Policy Manual, making notes and writing down new policy ideas for things I knew needed to change with the current times. My own office was directly above Paul's office and located on the second floor. My office door was adorned with my name in gold letters on one plaque and the *Director of Security* below my name on another plaque.

My desk was not as opulent as Paul's beautiful desk but was still impressive with its dark polished wood, and finished edging. My IBM Selectric typewriter sat on a pull-out shelf to my left, where I typed Memos, or various letters when necessary.

In the typewriter rested a page of my partially written policy on maintaining the new smoke detectors and *why* they were urgently needed.

I remember how surprised some of the staff were when they learned I could *type*. I'd hand them a typed Memo and they'd ask if I had a secretary. When I told them, no, that I typed the Memos myself, they were always surprised and it would make me chuckle. They must have thought I was just some dumb gumshoe detective, but even men could type and that was definitely me.

The five hundred smoke detectors I ordered through the purchasing executive, complete with five hundred sets of batteries, were now being installed by the maintenance crew starting at the top floor. One room at a time and one corridor at a time, they were going in. It was a relief! My newly written smoke detector policy dictated that each smoke detector in the guest corridors would be checked monthly and documented by clipboard and the mark of a ballpoint pen.

The policy also dictated that each guest room smoke detector would be checked daily to be in working order by the maid assigned to that room. Paul was horrified when I told him this would need to be done. It seemed like so much additional work and he didn't seem to understand *why* it was important.

Over the next few months, as happens, I soon discovered that the smoke detector batteries were occasionally stolen by guests and re-installed in their transistor radios, or "ghetto blasters" or used for other purposes. Such was the cost of doing business in a large big city hotel. The Executive Housekeeper seemed slightly annoyed as I inserted my new mandate on checking the batteries into her check-list for each maid.

"Make sure this gets done every day. It's really simple. They just press the little button and wait for the beep."

"Okay, Mr. DuPay. I'll have a meeting with the girls and let them know," she said.

It seemed I was irritating all the department heads as I cheerfully changed the way they had always done business. They were, however, learning the meaning of *Risk Management* and why it was important. While I knew they didn't like it, I also knew the future of the hotel would be better for all my new changes and I could handle being *The Bad Guy*.

Most of the old fogies in management hated change. *Damn this new guy anyway*, was the look I often saw on their faces when they saw me in the halls, particularly in the first few months I was employed as the Director of Security. Pinched up disapproving glances in my direction let me know I was doing my job and keeping the guests and employees *safe*. I didn't care if they called me a "rule crazy cop" behind my back, I was going to do my job.

After the smoke detectors were installed, I decided I would begin writing policy for the new Emergency Response Team I wanted. I knew management probably wouldn't care much for this new idea either but I was in charge now and *leading* was what I was born to do. I made the unpopular decisions and could handle the heat that went with it.

Having Lunch With Mom

It was around this time that I invited my mother, Clara DuPay, to meet me for lunch. I'd gone through a couple of challenging years and Mother had been justifiably worried about me. I had experienced a lot of trying times during the hard partying days of the late 1970s, which culminated with the murder, in mid-June of 1980, of my beautiful fiance Artent Thomas. After getting the job at the Benson and deciding to get clean and sober and go straight, my mother was proud of me, and I was proud of myself.

I invited Mother to lunch one afternoon, a few months after my promotion to Director of Security, and waited for her arrival. I put on one of my best suits, got my hair trimmed, and waited with a cup of hot coffee in hand, on the Mezzanine. I leaned over the railing, a favorite hangout, and watched the people mill about in the lounge below.

When I saw my petite mother wander in the front door, and look around to find me, I set the coffee down on a nearby table, walked to the top of the large staircase and waited until she saw me. Then I began my descent down what I sometimes called *The Grand Staircase*.

I indulged in a bit of theater as I walked down the staircase, because I wanted her to know I was okay. She had been disappointed when I resigned from PPB, after over 17 years, and now she could be proud of me again. I was the Director of Security for the Benson Hotel!

We would have a delicious lunch, with prime rib and salad for me, and cooked salmon and wild rice for her. I remember the big smile on her face as I made my way down the staircase, and how happy she was. "Oh Donnie!" she murmured under her breath, "I'm so happy to see you!"

While we ate our lunch, she listened intently as I told her all the ways the Benson needed to be upgraded and improved, along with the constant stressors of the job. This included the recent drama with Cheryl Falcone, and the pistol whipping and how the entire building had been surrounded by more than 20 police officers for four hours while crowds of Portlanders gathered around, gawking.

Mother seemed entertained by the stories I told her and reminded me how hard it was to manage a business, referring to the days when she and my father ran our family restaurant, *DuPay's Drive-in Restaurant and Cafe* on McLoughlin Boulevard. She reminded me of an incident that happened when the price of hamburger meat had gone up and she wasn't sure they could keep selling cheeseburgers. We laughed about the old days in the restaurant, with me working part time as a *Soda Jerk* with my Grant High School friends who came by regularly for a Brown Cow or a Green River. Seeing my mother again, after I'd survived so many painful and bewildering losses felt good. I knew my image had been restored in her eyes and that I no longer disappointed her. She was proud of me again.

Taking Full Advantage
of the Hotel Owner

In the meantime, I was set to annoy Chef Bauser yet again.

On my hourly inspection rounds I noticed that Bauser, and Jimmy Hufana, the Asian Sous Chef, and the other assorted line cooks ate their delectable lunch and dinners at a large round formal table in the basement kitchen. This beautiful table was set with white linen, cloth napkins, table silver reserved for banquet guests, a flower centerpiece and three or *four* bottles of wine with appropriate crystal wine glasses.

Wine? *While working?* It was like a free-for-all — food, booze, the works!

This elegant set-up left no doubt about the elite status enjoyed by Chef Bauser and his favored staff. The rest of us lesser mortals ate in the cafeteria on regular plates and silver that had seen better days in common banquet use. Those that supped at "the round table" drank freely of the wine as they enjoyed their meals and elegant desserts. I had two problems with this group of elites. Their table was set up in the main kitchen pathway, essentially blocking the fire escape route, *and* they were drinking while on DUTY. Clearly, this was forbidden by company policy, as signed by Paul, himself.

One afternoon after squeezing my way past their dinner table, yet again blocking the aisle and making it difficult for anyone to access the fire exit, I nearly spilled the Chef's glass of Chardonnay. Bauser gave me one of his dark annoyed looks as I passed by on my way to our boss's office. I was unmoved by his annoyed expression and did *not* apologize. Once there, I banged on Paul's door. After he opened the door, I found it best not to beat around the bush and came right at him with it, again choosing to be nothing but direct.

"Paul, the Chef and his cooks are blocking the kitchen fire escape route with their dining table, and they're drinking on duty. This is *against* policy." Paul let out a long audible sigh, slowly pushing himself back from his desk. "Well, I mean… that's how they've *always* done it, Don."

"This ritual has to stop and it has to stop now. The table is a fire hazard and against code." I stated. "I can't do anything about it just now," Paul said, sighing again. "Why not?" I asked. "I just chewed him out about being mouthy to the women. I can't do it right now, Don."

"Okay!" I replied, turning on my heel without further comment. Now, it was time for plan B. I sat at my desk for about a half hour letting my anger subside, ruminating and preparing for my next course of action. Suddenly, a brilliant plan came to mind and I smiled at the thought of it.

When I felt more sorry for Paul than frustrated with him, I stood up, left my office and walked immediately and leisurely to the Lobby Lounge. Once there, I sat at the bar and ordered a glass of red wine. Fritz, the Filipino bartender, who had worked at the hotel almost as long as Marty the PBX operator, looked at me confused, with wide eyes. He was clearly worried, but he poured the wine, anyway. I paid my bill, sipped half the wine and then casually walked back to my office. With the wine glass in hand, I sat at my desk, and waited, feeling smug.

Less than a half hour later I received a call on my radio. "Paul wants to see you in his office," Marty said. "Be right there!" I responded cheerfully, hopping out of my chair.

Now, the fun would begin. After strolling into Paul's office, I sat dutifully in front of the boss's desk waiting for what I knew was coming, a small smile on my face. Paul looked very uncomfortable, and I tried to maintain a blank face, though I did feel an overpowering desire to laugh.

"Don? Well, the front office manager said… she observed you drinking at the lobby lounge, and…the bartender also said you drank a glass of wine. Is that true?"

"Why, Yes, actually it *is* true!" I answered brightly, still keeping a semi-poker face."But staff can't drink on duty," Paul said in a desperate, thin whisper. It was then, I pulled rank, and I could tell he *knew* it was coming. I leaned forward, and scooted my chair closer to his desk. My poker face disappeared as I leaned into him and stared him straight in the eyes, intensely.

"You mean, I can't drink on duty, Paul?" I asked, stressing each word, while giving him something of the crazy eye.

"Right, you can't drink on… on duty…"

"But Chef Superstar, and his cook staff CAN drink on duty?!"

"Don…" Paul moaned miserably.

"It's your father, buying them all those expensive bottles of wine. That *they* drink during LUNCH? Every single working DAY? How would your Dad feel if I called him and told him what's going on in his very own hotel? Have you calculated the cost on a monthly basis? It goes into the thousands!"

Paul shifted in his chair, avoiding eye contact.

"At least I PAID for my drink, Paul!" I said. "Your own policy, likely written by your father, says NO ONE can drink while on duty. It doesn't say no one except the chef and his underlings!"

Pushing him harder now, I raised my voice and continued. "Do you know what could happen to you if OSHA knew your employees were not only drinking on duty but *also* blocking the fire escape route while *doing* it?

"Come on, Don?!"

"Do you know how easy it would be for them to be informed of this, as the way things have "always" been done?" I watched his face go ashen as he thought about what I'd just said. A viable risk had been explained to him and reality was sinking in.

"By allowing it and buying their wine too, *you* are personally complicit in *any* problem this midafternoon drinking causes. A fight, a kitchen fire, someone stumbling, falling and injuring themselves because they're drunk? That makes *you* personally *liable*! You are after all the General Manager of this hotel, right?"

As I hammered this point home, I could see the shadow of Daddy Himmelman looming disapprovingly in Paul's mind, wagging his finger at his son and saying: "I told you so! I told you so!"

Paul pushed back his leather executive chair, stood up and then stared down at the carpet for what seemed like a long while. When he finally had the courage to look me in the face his expression told me I had won this round, too. "I'll take care of it, Don," he said firmly. I looked at him for a brief moment, saying nothing. Then I left the room without further comment. Two more stupid and unnecessary risks, drinking on duty and blocking the basement fire exit route would soon be eliminated.

I didn't take it as another feather in my cap, but as a step *forward* in bringing the Benson closer to surviving a potential lawsuit and into the modern age of the 1980s. Okay, maybe I *was* feeling a little smug. I had just stuck another needle in that over-privileged, self-important, overblown cook's backside–but all for a good cause of course, which was hotel safety *and* the continued existence of the Benson Hotel!

My position allowed me to access all areas of the hotel from the laundry and housekeeping rooms on the top floor to Chef Bauser's sprawling basement kitchen and I made it my business to make sure all aspects of the operation of the hotel were done smoothly, safely *and* efficiently.

Hotel Theft was Rampant and Shameless

I sometimes paused to watch the ladies in housekeeping on the top floor operate the automatic bedsheet folding machine. Clean sheets arrived from the huge gas heated dryers via a conveyor belt which was fed into the folding machine. It automatically folded and stacked clean pink sheets for the next shift. It also stacked the clean pink bath and hand towels.

The Benson's pretty pink linen was often stolen by departing guests simply because it was pretty and pink. Management complained to me about the ongoing theft, but the same pink linen was sold in the gift store in the lobby. I asked Paul how I was supposed to tell the stolen pink towels from those purchased in the gift store? He just shook his head, grumbled about the stupid laws and agreed when I pointed out the legal problems this might cause. Eventually, the desirable pink linen was discontinued, but not until every guest and even the employees who wanted the stylish pink linen had all secreted away some for themselves.

It seemed to me that nearly every employee of the Benson hotel was stealing *something*. From linen, to silverware, (a fork here and a spoon there easily hidden in a pocket or purse after work) to bottles of expensive wine, and even gallons of ice cream from the kitchen, stolen at night by cooks, maids and janitors. Nothing was locked up anywhere and that fact seemed outrageous to me!

I knew I had to do something about the theft.

During the fall canning season I noticed that pounds of sugar, flour, cinnamon, nutmeg and other seasonings would just magically disappear from the unlocked bins in Chef Bauser's roomy kitchen. With all the plenty, it would be easy for employees to scoop a pound or two of the fine flour into a plastic bag, stuff it into their lunch box or purse and thereby cut down on their monthly grocery bill. But with so many employees stealing, it was costing the hotel a small fortune. The theft was rampant, and frustrating because of course, I could never seem to catch anyone in the act.

Part of my job as Director of Security for the Benson was minimizing theft. It was a constant battle. The Benson had at least 180 employees, perhaps more, including staffing for two restaurants, maids for 287 rooms, housemen, bellmen, front desk and office staff workers.

In my efforts to control theft, I conducted frequent and unannounced locker and bag inspections.

One afternoon, while inspecting lockers, I noticed two expensive bottles of Sokol Blosser red wine in a locker belonging to a London Grill waiter. Due to the constant theft of wine and other food items, I had decided the week before to set a trap in order to catch any thieves. This waiter had been on my radar for a long time. There was something about his attitude I just didn't like - something smug and entitled.

In my former profession, as a street cop and later, a police detective, I had learned a few tricks. One involved the usefulness of tracing powder. This is often called "visible thief detection powder," or "ultraviolet tracking powder." The powder is invisible but fluoresces purple under black light, in other words, ultraviolet light.

The day I found the wine in the waiters locker, (let's call him Rich) I had arranged an inspection of all employees leaving for the day. At quitting time, around five in the afternoon, the employees would exit through the Oak street side doors. I directed them to form a line and individually inspected their hands. I used a handheld fluorescent black light, shaped like a long tube, and made from metal and black plastic.

As several people passed the inspection, about 30, they were allowed to leave and walk out the doors. There were another 40-50 people yet to be inspected. After a couple of minutes, it was Rich's turn to be inspected. He was a white, dark-haired guy in his forties, not too tall and slightly overweight. As a longtime Benson employee he had gotten a little too comfortable in his job and I'd never liked his attitude.

Rich acted very surprised when his hands floresed a bright violet color under the black light.

When I saw Rich's hands glowing under the black light, I was furious. I gripped his right shoulder firmly, and pulled him out of the line. I immediately told him he was done. "You're fired for stealing! Let's go down to your locker so you can get your things!" Rich mumbled something about how he didn't do it and kept looking at his hands uncomprehendingly. What did his hands have to do with anything, he seemed to be wondering out loud?

When we got down to his locker, Rich slowly opened it, dreading the inevitable, I could tell. There were the two bottles of wine resting on the bottom area of the locker. Not only was the wine in his locker, a clear indication of theft, but both bottles had tracing powder on them. I shone the light over the bottles and then over his hands. Both the bottles and his hands glowed bright purple. It was then that Rich seemed to understand he was history at the Benson.

I stood by as Rich glumly cleaned out his locker and then I escorted him out of the building. At the door, I took the opportunity to tell him: "Don't ever come back here, not even to get a drink, or for food. And don't ask for a recommendation for another job. Because no one at the Benson will recommend a thief, and that's what you are!" After I threw Rich out, I walked to the basement kitchen, and approached Xavier Bauser, and told him: "You're going to be short a waiter at the London Grill, because I fired the guy for stealing wine."

I thought Xaiver would be more surprised than he was, but he didn't respond. He just scowled at me and turned on his heel, clip-clopping away in his wooden shoes. He mumbled something under his breath that I couldn't understand, because his thick accent muffled through his mustache but it was clear to me that Xaiver was not surprised. After speaking with him about the fired waiter, I returned to my office on the second floor and typed up a report for the boss, Paul, and for personnel and accounting.

The vast majority of Benson employees were good, honest and loyal people - they did not steal. But theft happened regularly and I did my best to curb it. When word got around that Don DuPay, former police detective, was using tracing powder to locate thieves, I could swear that some of the department heads treated me with a little more respect. It was a "policey" thing to do, but it was also effective.

Since I now had the ear of the purchasing agent, Janet, (who had helped me curb Chef Superstar's nasty habit of bullying women employees) and putting something of a stop to his verbal abuse, I was kept apprised of what the kitchen was regularly missing. Janet noticed she was having to spend far too much of the hotel's money replacing all the stolen food stores of flour, sugar, butter, eggs and spices. I realized there were so many security issues at the Benson, it would take a while to address them all. But I was tenacious and beginning with one concern at a time, I addressed each issue with kitchen theft.

After checking the guest corridors from housekeeping down to the front desk, I would occasionally relax for a moment in one of the big easy chairs. With a mug of hot coffee, I would sit in the lobby and watch the people coming and going through the front door. Because the Benson is located on SW Broadway in the heart of downtown Portland, and only a few blocks from skid row, the occasional ne'er-do-well, dirty, scruffily dressed lost soul would sneak past the doorman into the lobby to pan handle, begging the wealthy guests for money or to try to sell a few wilted Portland roses in exchange for a dollar or two.

Me at the Benson in the early 80's. Photo courtesy of Scott Allen Tice.

Many of the guests, in an effort to get rid of the person, would quickly hand them a five or ten dollar bill, to help hurry them on their way, but their generosity could create a problem if allowed to continue. If I saw the person first, I would meet them at the door with a friendly smile, turn them around by their elbow and escort them back out onto the street. I made a point of politely ignoring their protestations that they weren't doing anything, wherein they would whine: "I ain't doin' nuffin! I was gonna buy me a drink!" or some other lie or excuse. If I was not readily available, the front office clerks would call me on the radio and alert me to the presence of an "unwanted" and I would come down from my office on the second floor and deal with them.

I often found them wandering around and annoying guests with their life story and why they needed a perfect sum of money, generally five or ten dollars, to buy another bottle of gut-rot booze. They generally favored fortified wine, which is a distilled spirit that has brandy added to it. Fortified wine was especially popular among homeless transients because it was stronger and got them drunk faster. It dulled any pain they might be in, although it did give them "the wine shits" as PPB detectives and I used to call it.

Sometimes the bellmen would escort the bums out, but they felt more comfortable calling me, knowing I had been a police detective and had no problem being assertive and politely telling people that they had to leave. The Benson Hotel was an elegant place and an "unwanted" was generally removed, as pleasantly and as quietly as possible. The more stubborn and intoxicated ones a little less pleasantly, sometimes forcefully ushered out the side door onto SW Oak street with a stern warning not to come back.

I Often Reflected on How Lucky I Was

During those times I sat in the lobby, with a cup of hot coffee in my hands, during a break, I was always amazed at how beautiful and elegant my surroundings were. The walls were paneled with rare Circassian walnut imported from Russia. It was a rich, warm brown, highly polished, and elegantly veined wood. The Austrian crystal chandeliers were large and ornate, looking like they belonged in a French palace. They hung, drifting imperceptibly from the decorated ceiling by imposing brass chains, as the air moved gently in the room. The flame shaped electric bulbs reflected light from the sparkling crystals, which made the crystals look rather like backlit diamonds.

The floors were highly polished European marble as was the check-in counter. I always marveled at how Simon Benson, the hardworking logger and lumberman was able to visualize and create something as impressive and elegant as this hotel that bore his name.

I realized I had a plum job as the Director of Security. There was only *one* Benson Hotel and there was only *one* Director of Security, and that was me. I felt blessed once again to be enjoying a position of authority, in a similar manner as when I'd been a police detective for PPB in the 1960s and 1970s.

It felt good to be in charge and though there were legal problems to solve, and many feathers yet to ruffle, I knew I was in my element making those tough decisions. It became clear my forte was solving problems, leading others to perform *their* duties better, and gradually soothing the hurt feelings of the department heads I still had to confront about doing their jobs more effectively.

The Eruption of Mt. Saint Helens

On the historic Morning of May 18, 1980, I was blessed to be in the right place at the right time. Every morning on my top-to-bottom inspection of the hotel, I checked the rooftop, which offered an exhilarating panoramic view of the city of Portland from twelve floors up.

I often visited the Benson's rooftop in an effort to clear my mind and come up with plans to improve guest safety, in case of a fire, which was something I worried about regularly. Because it was a really good place to go and think alone, my problem solving abilities were often quite good when I was up there, standing alone with a mug of hot coffee in my hand and scanning the world below.

In time, I became more friendly with the Portland Fire Bureau's Fire Marshal. He was a friendly man who had seen it all, and we were on a first name basis. Together we decided it would be a good idea to arrange to land a helicopter on the roof, if necessary, to evacuate guests who might seek refuge there in the event of a fire. We regularly bounced ideas off each other when we met for lunch.

That morning in May, I was alerted on my radio by Marty that Mount St. Helens had just begun to erupt. I was on the roof already, looking south when Marty called, and after I turned around, I stood mesmerized watching the huge clouds of thick grey smoke billowing skyward. The smoke and ash continued to erupt into a lovely mushroom cloud, which appeared motionless, with hardly any movement at all. Gradually, I could feel the ash burning my exposed forearms. It was still hot.

Wow, I thought, as it sprinkled on my skin!

It was an eerie feeling watching ash fall from the sky and feeling it burn my skin and collect in my hair and on the tip of my nose. I watched as it began coating the hotel roof and Broadway Street below. Other staff joined me, hearing that I was on the roof, for now *everyone* wanted to see what was happening from the top of the Benson. We formed a small crowd of people, as we stood around, watched and marveled from the top of the Benson Hotel, voicing our collective opinion that we hoped it would soon stop *and* that it was a once in a lifetime experience.

I watched for what seemed like a long time, feeling the sting of hot ash slowly settle on my arms, and drift away. I realized as we stood watching what seemed like fire and brimstone belching up from the bowels of hell, that people were almost certainly dying.

A total of 57 people would be killed in all and I felt a definite yet removed feeling of loss later that day when I watched the KGW News and the devastation was more fully revealed. There was also the loss of the eccentric old man, Harry Randall Truman, a man born in 1896, who was the owner and operator of the Mount St. Helens Lodge. He had stubbornly refused to leave the mountain even after evacuation orders were made, instead choosing to stay on with his cats to perish in what scientists said would have been an instant death due to heat shock.

Mount St. Helens and nearby Spirit Lake were a resort area, and generally populated by campers and hikers and I knew that now they had been obliterated, along with any gawkers, if they had not evacuated in time.

The cars trying to navigate SW Broadway were turning on their headlights as clouds of smoke and ash blotted out the remaining sunlight. It seemed like it was suddenly dusk but it was still early in the day, so there was a strange feeling of foreboding as well. I felt as though I had witnessed an Atomic Bomb explode as fully half of the upper portion of the huge mountain had simply disappeared in the blink of an eye. Later, news reports told of the disappearance of Spirit Lake and thousands of trees being blown down, simply flattened, blocking the nearby Toutle River.

When the eruption was over, city crews swept up piles and piles of powdery ash, thousands of pounds of it, loading the muck into bags and discarding it in large garbage trucks. Within a couple of days, word got out that "entrepreneurs" were collecting the ash, believing it would become valuable years later and pouring it into Mason jars to save. We all chuckled at the *kooks* who were doing this.

This did, of course, come to pass years later, when the ash did become valuable, and people sold it in little bottles, marking it as "Genuine ash," from Mount St. Helens "once in a lifetime" blast. They sold it much like beach sand is sold in small bottles in Honolulu. Ceramic figures made of the melted ash appeared and were sold by street vendors weeks later and I recall Tee shirts appeared as well, that read: "Spirit Lake Water Ski Team!"

My view of the landscape from the top of the Benson Hotel would never be the same after that day. What a sight it had been. Indeed, what a sight! It was a day I will remember forever, etched in my memory in vibrant color, detail and emotion.

The Wet Bar & the Fire Escape Dilemma

One of the best things about working at the Benson was getting to see the famous celebrities as they checked in to stay for a day or a week, or a month. Rich Little, the renowned comic and impressionist, performed one summer evening in the early 1980s in the main ballroom, which was called the Mayfair

Room, for a banquet event of several hundred high-rollers.

Sou Chef, Jimmy Hufana was an artist and incredibly skilled at carving ice sculptures and once created a stunning dolphin rising from a foaming surf. A huge block of solid ice had been delivered to the kitchen and I was able to watch Jimmy create this dolphin with an ice pick and a small electric chain-saw. He was amazing and I felt fortunate to watch him create such fleeting and beautiful art. The sculpture would be delivered to the banquet room and lighted from underneath with colored lights, in pink and purple. Jimmy's creations were always stunning but short lived works of art.

When large events in our two ballrooms were scheduled, I usually returned to the hotel in the evenings, after I had clocked out, to see what was going on and certainly to see Rich Little during his stay. Little performed flawless impressions of Johnny Carson, Jack Benny and of course his famous impression of President Richard Nixon.

The event with Rich Little would also be a headbutting competition between myself and Freddie, the prim and proper Catering Manager, responsible for setting up the event and then of course, Chef Xavier Bauser.

The menu for this gala included exotic cheeses on tiny, delicate "water" and "cream" crackers, and raw Pacific oysters on the half shell. They were usually seasoned with lime and lemon juice, or Mignonette Sauce and Ponzu, a Japanese soy sauce. There were generous slices of Spinach Quiche, Bauser's special twice baked potatoes with Tillamook cheddar cheese topping, mountains of green leafy salad with luscious dressings, thirty cases of the best wine, a full bar and huge chunks of perfectly cooked prime rib.

This was a major event serving hundreds of folks and costing thousands of dollars. Everything had to be *Benson Hotel* perfect at this $50 per plate event. By the time I arrived at the hotel that evening, the ballroom was already a hubbub of activity, with people milling around everywhere. The light from the crystal chandeliers was turned down low and the stage, though still unoccupied, was bathed with diffused pastel floodlighting. At least thirty servers with white blouses and black skirts had nervous smiles pasted frozenly on their faces. The sound of wine corks popping combined with the sounds of continuous conversation and tinkling cocktail glasses filled with ice.

I had seen the Mayfair Room set up for events exactly like this on previous occasions. The dinner tables were round and seated six guests at each table with room for a floral centerpiece, linen napkins, proper silverware and water and wine glasses. The tables had been pushed closer together than normal, leaving barely enough room for the servers to move about with wine bottles and barely enough room for guests to push back their chairs in their quest to search for nearby restrooms.

As my eyes became accustomed to the dim lighting I noticed an additional five or six dining tables, far more than usual, which had been placed around the edge of the room. The place was crowded and I was becoming concerned.

With each table having multiple candles flickering, plus the heat of so many bodies, the air conditioning was not keeping up, and it started feeling warm, close and stuffy. The overly busy servers were barely keeping up, uncorking and pouring wine, and I could see fine beads of sweat on their foreheads as they passed me with an acknowledging nod.

After a few moments of standing there, I saw Freddie working her way through the maze of tables as if she wanted to speak to me. As she got within ear shot, she impatiently pushed a full bottle of wine at me and said: "We need some help. You'll have to pour wine!" Her demand was brusque, familiar and *inappropriate*. I gently deflected the green bottle of *Pinot Noir* with the back of my hand, refusing to take it. "I'm sorry, but that's not something I can do," I said quietly but firmly. As she looked at me, dumbfounded, I positioned myself next to her, standing to her right, so I could get a full view of all the people milling about. It was then that I patiently explained that I would *not* be serving wine for two reasons.

"First of all, it would be as inappropriate for the Director of Security of the Benson Hotel to serve wine as it would be for *you*, the Catering Manager, to clean bathrooms. The second reason I can't serve wine is that anyone who serves alcohol *must* have an *Oregon Liquor Servers Permit* in order to do so, and that is something I do not possess. So I will not be in a position to serve wine," I concluded, politely.

Freddie was speechless. She stared at me in disbelief. She was not used to being told no. Even though I'd been on the job a couple of years, to her, I was still "the new guy." Apparently, she felt she could start bossing me around if she felt like it. She was wrong.

When Freddie saw I was not kidding and had no intention of serving anyone anything, she turned angrily in military fashion and stormed off. She almost lost her grip on the wine bottle she carried as she stumbled in her haste to get away from me.

Because she had a short haircut, with clipped dark hair, I could see that her ears had turned bright red as she disappeared into the crowd. What was she thinking, I wondered, by even daring to ask me to pour wine? That was not part of my job description. This was the first time Freddie had encountered me in my official capacity and I had definitely ruffled her feathers. As it turned out, it wouldn't be the last time.

Since Rich Little wouldn't appear on stage until all the food courses had been delivered, I decided to get a few minutes of fresh air. This would allow the surprise of the behind-the-scenes drama of crowded rooms and Freddie's wine pouring demand subside.

I leaned against the wall outside the hotel by the Oak street exit which was near the freight elevator. I caught the faint evening breeze and recalled my short interaction with Miss Fuss-budget, the Catering Manager. I shook my head and chuckled, remembering the astonished look on her face and took a last deep breath before stepping inside the big glass doors with the gold lettering that read, *The Benson Hotel*. Once inside I could faintly hear the MC introducing Rich Little and I hurried up the grand marble stairway to the Mayfair Room, not wanting to miss his wonderful celebrity impersonations.

As I strolled in, I could see the guests were laughing at this funny man as he went through his comedy routine. If you weren't looking at him you'd swear Jack Benny was in the room, making fun of Johnny Carson, or vice versa. But my job was to watch the crowd, as much as I would rather have only watched Rich Little.

As my eyes again became accustomed to the dim light, I started counting the dinner tables. Then I started to count the number of guests. I calculated there were between 340 and 350 dinner guests. This was far too many people in the room and it put us over the fire marshal's occupancy permit of only 300. I understood why this was happening–because at $50 a plate the room would take in several thousand more dollars in food revenue sales even before counting the take from selling whiskey and other alcohol like wine, gin, champagne and vodka.

I slowly worked my way around the outside edge of the busy room, smiling politely at the guests who made eye contact with me. Finally, I squeezed by the last table near the main fire exit, stunned at what I saw.

The exit was totally blocked by a portable wet bar!

I couldn't believe what I was seeing and immediately felt the back of my neck heat up. I frowned at the two uniformed bartenders, shaking my head disapprovingly. They were busily filling glasses with ice. I demanded to know who had decided it was a good idea to block the main fire exit at a crowded, over-capacity event.

"Who in hell approved the location of this wet bar?! You realize this blocks the fire exit?!"

They both gave me a deer in the headlights look, before one of them sputtered: "The boss told us to put it here. That it would be okay." I wondered if the boss was Bauser or Freddie. "Which boss?" I asked, disgusted. "Well, the Catering Manager. She said it would be alright." I was furious as I stood contemplating my next move. How could the entire catering staff be so stupid as to *block* a fire exit? How could Freddie, or Bauser be so unaware of simple fire safety?

Was I the *only* person who thought of such things?

An overturned candle on a table, could catch the nearby heavy draperies on fire in an instant, which would quickly navigate toward the ceiling. People would jump away from the flames, someone would yell: "Fire! Fire!" and hotel guests would be crushed against each other in the ensuing stampede, trying to get past the manmade obstruction, and then *maybe* to safety.

The gruesome details of the notorious 1911 *Triangle Shirtwaist Factory Fire* in Manhattan instantly came to my mind. I knew of the 146 young women, and underage girls, mostly penniless European immigrants who had perished. They died because there were only *two* exits, and two elevators, located on each end of the ninth floor.

The greedy owners, Isaac Harris and Max Blanck had locked the fire escape exit doors to prevent women from leaving work without first having their bags checked to prevent fabric theft. This meant that the Greene Street stairway was blocked by flames, and the Washington Place Stairway was locked to prevent anyone from leaving early.

The women regularly worked 16 hour shifts, with only one

short half hour for a lunch break. This endless work earned them the enviable sum of seven dollars a week while they continued to live in abject poverty. Dozens of women died in the fire and there were dozens of women who died after jumping to their deaths, from the 8th and 9th floors in an effort to escape the flames.

The New York Triangle Fire was one of the worst fires in American history and I understood how easily a devastating fire could happen at the Benson Hotel if fire safety rules were routinely ignored. People would die if things didn't change, with dozens of lawsuits filed against the hotel for negligence. Why was I the *only* person to think about these potential dangers?

I looked around the Mayfair Room for Freddie and seeing her, I strode over to her and gently pulled her aside by the elbow and out of the earshot of the other guests. I didn't want anyone to overhear the danger they had all been placed in by our unprofessional and naive staff. And Freddie (though she was clearly no smarter than Chef Bauser) could *not* be humiliated in public by the tongue lashing I intended to give her.

"Freddie, you *must remove* that bar station from the fire exit immediately! Just what the hell is going on here? Why do you think you can *do* that?" I demanded. I looked her in the eyes and waited for a response. Again, she was filled with resentment towards me and glared up at me. "We put it there so the servers wouldn't have to cross the *entire* room going to the main bar in the back kitchen! I can't move it, NOW!" she responded.

"Why not?"

"We're just too busy!"

"Let me put it to you another way. You *have* to move it out of the fire escape, and that's what I'm telling you. I'm the Director of Security and *I* am telling you it presents a clear danger, goes against Fire Code and must be removed. *NOW.*"

I stared her down, calmly waiting for her response. There was no response. She turned on her heels again with that about-face, dismissive military manner of hers and headed directly for the serving kitchen where Chef Bauser was still slicing up his delectable prime rib. I followed her and stood a few feet away, watching.

I could hear her voice, as she made no attempt to lower it. "The security guy over there?" she said, with a condescending nod in my direction, "HE says we hafta move our portable bar out of the fire escape! But you *know* we're too busy right now. We'll tear it down after the event is over, like always!"

It was clear Freddie was seeking confirmation from who she considered to be her real boss. But while Chef Bauser was the "boss" of the kitchen, I was the "boss," of the general security and safety of the *entire* hotel, and all that that entailed. Freddie looked over at me and then back at the Chef thinking this time she could overrule me and that Bauser would back her up.

I could see, she meant to challenge my authority, so I knew I had to deal with that challenge in immediate fashion. Chef Bauser was busy, and preoccupied cutting meat, and fed up I could tell because again there I was changing the rules from how things had "always" been done, to how they *should* be done. He stood looking over at me, and I could tell he was deciding whether to approach me and take me on, or to ignore Freddie's complaint.

I beat him to it as I strode over and stood my ground. Without waiting for either of them to speak, I addressed Bauser directly, ignoring Freddie. "We are currently way over room capacity, which as you should know is 300. You simply cannot block a fire escape for any reason, not now, not *ever*." Bauser remained silent, glowering over at me as he continued to cut slabs of prime rib.

A long pause ensued, as Chef Bauser stopped cutting meat, and angrily glanced at the bar and then back at me. Then he went back to carving slices of prime rib, and I could see he was trying to decide on an answer, and waiting to see if I'd back down. The silence lengthened and I became angry. They were defying me and not allowing me to do my job.

"Move that Goddamned bar or I'll move it myself!" I threatened quietly.

I waited but still Bauser would not speak. Receiving no answer from his Royal Chef-ness, I leaned over the carving table and spoke very near his ear to make sure he understood me. "If you don't move that bar now, I'll have the Fire Marshal drop by and shut this little party down. It's all on YOU now, boss!" I said mustering up my best sarcasm. "Do as I say or you'll embarrass the hotel with a huge fine from the fire department. I know the guy by name and I *will* call him! It would make the papers. Do you want that?"

Another succulent slab of prime rib was being viciously attacked by Bauser's sharp carving knife as reality set in. He real-ized he had been defeated in the name of hotel safety and com-mon sense. He glared at me, twitching his little Swiss mustache and looking for all the world like the Pillsbury Dough-Boy in his two foot tall, white starched hat.

Without uttering a word, Bauser looked at Freddie, and nod-ded firmly, in the direction of the wet bar, telling her with the gesture to comply with my demand. He then ignored me and continued angrily slicing prime rib without another word.

Freddie was furious. Without looking at me, she made her about-face, tight-lipped and angry and stomped away. In a few minutes, after two bartenders moved the portable bar, the fire exit was finally free of any obstruction and I knew the guests would be safe.

I walked down the exit and onto the street, inhaling more fresh air. I removed my name tag from my suit coat handkerchief pocket and walked a block north to the notorious Mary's Club and ordered a whiskey and Seven-Up in a bucket glass. Mary's Club was a popular Portland skid row bar and strip club, locat-ed only a block north from the posh Benson Hotel but worlds away in terms of clientèle.

It was made up of working men, skid row transients and wom-en with too much makeup and reeking of cheap perfume. I loosened my tie and breathed in the noisy, smoky atmosphere. Somehow, I felt right at home and it was a relief to be away from the constant stressors of the Benson Hotel and its upkeep.

Butting heads with stupid people had given me another head-ache but I knew I had saved the hotel yet again. After the first whiskey, I decided to stay awhile and ordered another. I took my tie completely off and shoved it in my jacket pocket. I unbuttoned my shirt one more button, pushed my sleeves to my elbows and took to noticing the pretty girls.

I had been single way too long after losing my beautiful fiance, Artent Thomas. She was viciously murdered in the middle of 1980 while on a short trip to Seattle. Artent was Black, small boned and thin, stunningly attractive and had bumped into an old boyfriend on the trip to Seattle. This man decided he would rather murder Artent rather than see her marry a white man, who used to be a cop. *Me*. He lured her to a city park to sit and talk and ambushed her instead, raping and murdering her with a knife. Her horrible death devastated me and I grieved for months. But I had to move on. I needed to think about re-entering the land of the living. Though I was taking my time and still grieving the horrific loss of Artent, only 29-years-old when she was taken from me, I had to continue trying to live.

Later, after going home, I showered away the faint residue of cheap perfume from Mary's Club and finally crashed in bed. The next morning, I dressed in a three piece suit, and drove to work. I had a pitcher of coffee sent up to my office, with a warm croissant, delivered by room service, and with a fresh sheet of paper in my electric typewriter I began pounding the keys.

I was irritated that I had to write more policy, to ensure the safety of hotel guests. But I would. That was part of my job, and so in black and white, plain English wording I composed the new policy improvement. Something which should have been so common sense had to be explained by me, as if I were teaching a bunch of grammar school children the basics of fire safety. "Number one," I began writing, "under no circumstances will a Benson Hotel fire exit ever be blocked for any reason during any banquet events, by either the head Chef or any bartenders. Number two, it is the policy of the Benson Hotel to never exceed the room occupancy limits set by the fire marshal."

I included a few more details and then dropped by Paul Mannerly's office and had him sign off on the new policy after telling him about the events of the night before and my conflict with Freddie and Chef Bauser. Paul concluded the meeting with a brief but knowing smile, as he stood up to shake my hand. It seemed to me that Paul derived some real satisfaction that by signing the new policy order he too was asserting his authority over the fearsome, temperamental yet brilliant, Chef Bauser and that made me smile.

There was no more conversation about the behind-the-scenes-drama of the last evening's event in the Mayfair Room and with Paul's initials, my policy became the new hotel *law*. I entered it into the official policy notebook which I kept in my office, and sent copies to all department heads with a signature line near the bottom of the page, which they were required by law to sign and return to me.

Freddie, and Chef Bauser, particularly, had to sign off on the new policy and return it to me post haste. I knew it must have irked them no end, but that was how it was done. After I'd completed this small but important chore, and given myself a little time to gloat—that pure common sense had triumphed over the dogma of which lawsuits were made—it was time for lunch and I was eager to get to the employee cafeteria for the still delicious Mayfair Room leftovers.

Leftovers From the Benson were a Feast

All food left over from a large event would be served at the next opportunity in the cafeteria for us lesser mortals. There was still plenty of prime rib for everyone, a table of exotic cheeses, like Stilton, Brie and some unusual German and Swiss cheeses, like Appenseller cheese, a Swiss cheese and a German cheese, Allgäuer Emmentaler, which are both known for their spicy and nutty flavors, respectively. There was a huge bowl of colorful green salad and some excellent cheesy Quiche Lorraine, along with a lot of succulent fruit sliced on serving plates.

The ice dolphin that Jimmy Hufana had created had melted to a mere minnow, splashing in a pool of water and would be further melted into nothingness by the dishwashing staff. The leftovers were a win-win situation for hotel management. The food had already been paid for by the guests, and Sou Chef Jimmy Hufana, whose responsibility it was to provide for the employees, didn't have to cook anything special for several days as nothing was ever wasted.

Everything came down to the cafeteria, except the many half-full left over bottles of wine. The bottles of wine never seemed to make it, they just disappeared into the ether somewhere. I didn't care where the half-full wine bottles went, or who drank the wine, because it too had been *paid* for. Though drinking on duty was still against the rules, officially at least.

The cafeteria was lovingly supervised by Lillian, a woman in her early 60s with dyed red hair, which was always wrapped in a hairnet as required by the Health Department. Lillian would seat herself on her stool behind the serving line and make sure that each employee received a generous helping, and a kind word. "How's your day going?" she would ask, or "You look too thin. Here, have an extra piece of cheesecake."

Lillian saw her job as being the one who took care of the "little people," at the hotel. That meant the dishwashers, the janitors, the maids, the servers and even me, whom she often impishly referred to as "that security guy." There were a few caring and compassionate employees of long standing at the hotel. They called themselves the "BH employees," which meant "before Himmelman."

The Emergency Response Team

In time I began to notice that Paul seemed to be enjoying his job more fully since I had taken some of the pressure off. He must have realized that his father's hotel was a lot less likely to get in serious legal trouble with *me* overseeing security and making myself unpopular with some of the chefs and other staff and managerial employees in my quest to make sure the Benson was safe. Truth be told, I knew Paul was glad of my presence at the Benson. I could be the Bad Guy, and *he* would have less hassle to deal with.

I was nowhere close to being finished making important changes and improvements, though. There was still a lot of work to be done. After numerous meetings with one of several fire marshals, I devised a plan to create the Benson Hotel's first ever *Emergency Response Team*. Since there were employees in charge of the hotel 24 hours a day, I would use them as members of the ERT. The ERT was an innovative idea but one that I felt was a *must* to maintain hotel safety for all guests and employees.

The team would consist of at least one and usually two women from the front office check in counter. They would arrive at the emergency location with two sets of master keys, portable radios, fire extinguishers and a first aid kit. Joining the team was at least one maintenance man, arriving with his portable radio, master keys, another fire extinguisher and a fire ax in case the team needed to make a forced entry into a locked room.

The on-duty Bellman would complete the team with his portable radio, a fire extinguisher and an additional first aid kit. Several practice runs at various hours of the day and night got the team used to working together, but their arrival time was, at first, in excess of five minutes. Even though the hotel was twelve stories, thirteen if you count the roof-top, and sprawled over an entire half a city block, a *five minute* response time was simply unacceptable to me.

We had to do better!

From my experience as a street cop and police detective, I knew that people could die in five minutes. I further knew that repeated practice would cut the time to an acceptable *three* minutes and so I began a series of unannounced fire drills to keep the team on their toes. I learned through the grapevine that some of the staff were beginning to call me a "tyrant for safety" and an annoying, (formerly employed with PPB) "rule crazy cop."

They were right. And I didn't care who knew it.

In collusion with the on-duty PBX operator, Marty, I would instruct her to call the frontdesk radios and report the smell of smoke on say, the seventh floor South at any given time of the day or night. The other responders would hear the radio call and go immediately to seven South. After a month or so of regular drilling I was happy to report to Paul Mannerly that our Emergency Response Team could reach any point in the hotel within three minutes with fire extinguishers, master keys, first aid kits and an ax at the ready. With his approval, I then wrote *new* hotel policy on both the overall makeup and duties of the ERT, typing it up myself on my handy electric typewriter.

I was beginning to breathe better, knowing the hotel was moving forward to a new era of professional responsibility to the guests, and overall safety. The Benson Hotel was steadily moving out of the dark ages.

But there was one problem. With regard to the ERT, it was the ho-hum factor. Just another fire drill they thought. "Let's get it over with—it's not real—Don's just messin' with us again," I could hear them saying. I felt we needed a little more realism. It would be good for them, so I decided to provide it myself. One night at about three am, I arrived surreptitiously at the hotel and told only the night shift PBX operator of my plan. I decided on having my "emergency" on nine North, near the luxury suite that had once been occupied by Cheryl Falcone and the floor that was long rumored to be "haunted" by a ghost.

I lit a folded newspaper on fire and waved it around the corridor and in front of the ninth floor elevator lobby. Then I told PBX to report a possible fire on nine North and waited. This time the ho-hum group of first responders filed out of the elevator and as they did so, *they* smelled smoke. Their looks changed from cavalier disinterest and *Let's get this over with*, to fear and concern in about *one* second.

I know this because I was lurking down the hall, waiting for them and watching them from a discreet distance. I could almost feel their buttholes pucker in apprehension when they filed out of the elevator. That is until they saw me with my stopwatch, standing down the hall. Then they began berating me under their breath. *"You scared us to death, Don!"* the Bellman said angrily. *"We thought it was just another drill!"* he concluded with growing irritation.

I ignored their comments and complaints and announced: *"Yeah, but you arrived here in three minutes flat! Congratulations team! You did a great job!"* I cheerfully slapped the grumpy Bellman on the back, a dedicated worker named Glenn, who prided himself on perfect attendance and laughed in spite of myself. It was good for them to be challenged, and years from now, they'd always remember the paces I put them through.

I now felt that the hotel was safe enough for me to personally stay overnight, without risking life or limb. Except for still having to push the dresser in front of the room door because no one knew how many keys were floating around Portland. I felt guests would be *fairly* safe while staying at the Benson. But I was still formulating a long-term plan for guest room key control and that was my *next* chore.

Key control would take some time for me to figure out and would be a major change for these collective despots of hospitality who didn't want their routines messed with. People naturally hate change, especially if it means they have to put forth more *effort* in their daily responsibilities and duties. I knew there was an army of lawyers in Portland just waiting for a nice juicy hotel like the Benson to screw up in any number of ways, including the possibility of some night a fire breaking out in a smoldering cloud of foul smelling smoke.

I would not allow it. The Benson Hotel was a jewel and it was *my* job to protect it.

Getting to Know a Few Interesting Celebrities

Have you ever noticed that the celebrities you see on TV look a lot different in person? Perhaps when you stand in line for an autograph and see them up close, you get a better view. I loved that part of my job, getting to see the stars and the rich and famous while they stayed, "at The Benson of course!"

One afternoon, I was sitting in the lobby, people watching and making sure "unwanted" winos, panhandlers or prostitutes did not become a nuisance. On that day, I was lucky enough to be there when Gladys Knight and the Pips checked in. I thought Gladys was as cute as a bug's ear and was amazed to see she was in fact so incredibly petite. She was talking on the guest phone as she stood on her tip-toes to reach the signature card placed in front of her. "Where am I?" she asked her friend on the telephone. "Why, I'm at the Benson of course!"

I had to stop and think for a moment. Where had I heard that before? It seemed I'd heard it so many times from other guests that there was a feeling of déjà vu when she said it. Gladys was wearing a blue satin blouse and tight black satin pants, heavy eye makeup and bright red lipstick. The Pips were dressed in shiny blue slacks and jackets and seemed twice as tall as Gladys. She looked adorable, and I was in love with her for the rest of the day.

Out of town basketball teams also often stayed at the Benson. I remember Kareem Abdul-Jabbar of the Los Angeles Lakers exiting the guest elevator. He had to bend over to keep from bumping his head. He then crossed the lobby looking for all the world like a gangly spider or a skinny puppet on a string. It seemed that his legs went on forever and his long arms appeared to hang almost to the floor. He walked spider-like, and was the opposite of the graceful Kareem I remembered seeing on TV as he glided around while playing basketball, clearly in his element on the court. He appeared much taller in person than on TV and thinner too, to the point of looking emaciated. I remember he was quiet, kept to himself, always seemed to have a book in his hand and was soft spoken and polite.

One morning, sometime in 1980 or early 1981, shortly after I arrived for work, I walked down the carpeted stairway to the London Grill. It would be an hour or two before "the Grill" opened for lunch, and the breakfast crowd was gone. However, sitting in the far corner watching the staircase were two guys dressed in suits. They each held an Uzi machine gun resting on their lap.

Eating at the table behind them was none other than Moshe Dayan, (1915-1981) the Israeli military leader and politician. He had been commander of the Jerusalem front in the 1948 Arab–Israeli War, and Chief of Staff for the Israel Defense Forces during the 1956 Suez Crisis. He was also Defense Minister during the Six-Day War in 1967, and became a worldwide symbol of the new state of Israel. I recognized him from his famous eye patch which covered his destroyed left eye. Dyan barely looked up at me as he ate his poached eggs, with coffee and orange juice. His Israeli bodyguards nodded to me in formal acknowledgement as they sat near him, upright and alert.

I smiled faintly, and nodded politely, feeling uncomfortable with their gaze and the machine guns resting in their laps and kept walking, disappearing from view as I walked into the kitchen. Their eyes followed me making sure I was not a threat, and their Uzi's reminded me that Israel was always in some kind of conflict for one reason or another and they were serious people who demanded respect.

Bob Dylan Looked Like a Bum

Singer and musician Bob Dylan was another celebrity who nearly made my jaw drop as I watched him amble across the lobby to the check in counter. He looked like death warmed over, was pasty pale, with greasy dark hair that was tousled, overgrown and encrusted with dandruff. He had a scruffy beard, and was dressed from head to toe in all black, which constituted an ill fitting, dirty black jacket and dusty rumpled slacks that looked like he'd been wearing them for a month.

From my years experience as a cop Dylan looked *exactly* like a junkie to me. Ironically, I would come to find out later that he was a junkie while he stayed at the Benson Hotel. Dylan was accompanied by a little man, some kind of yapping assistant who held a sheaf of papers in his arms, talking a mile a minute, but much better dressed. Dylan's minion looked like he might belong at the Benson, but not Dylan.

Dylan walked along as if in a trance, just going through the motions. He looked like some of the "unwanted" lost souls I continually escorted out the side door onto Oak street with a smile and a pat on the shoulder. I knew Dylan was a famous celebrity, but seeing him in person, I wouldn't have paid ten dollars to see him perform. He looked like a bum and I was not impressed. If *he* didn't have more regard for his own personal hygiene and the state of his clothing, why would I want to see him perform his music?

Wandering the Hall
& Looking for a Piano

On another night, I was once again in the right place at the right time. It was in the quiet of the evening, sometime in the early 1980s and my shift was ending. I locked my office door on the second floor and walked down the long corridor to its far south end. My plan was to leave by the second floor fire exit onto Stark Street. I often entered and exited the hotel surreptitiously to keep the employees unsure if I was around or not, and keep them on their toes. They were never sure if "the security guy" was in the hotel or not as I appeared at all hours of the day and night, and from all locations.

Wandering down the corridor toward me I saw a middle-aged man, with thinning grey hair, his hands stuffed in his pockets, looking at the beautiful wallpaper and muttering to himself, as he still hadn't seen me. As we got closer to each other I thought he looked familiar and since he seemed lost, I asked him if I could help him, pointing to my black and gold name tag. "I'm on staff here," I explained. "Can I help you find something?" "I'm looking for a piano," he replied simply. I was more confused now than ever as most guests wandering the corridors were looking for an ice machine, or a candy or cigarette vending machine or the restrooms. I had never been asked for a piano before. Still he looked familiar. "Do I… know you?" I asked hesitantly.

"I'm Victor Borge!" he explained cheerfully, seeing that I was confused. "I play the piano and I have a concert tomorrow, so I need to practice." Then it hit me. He looked familiar because my Dad had taken me to see Victor Borge in concert when I was a high school kid in the 1950s. He was *the* Victor Borge, concert pianist and comedian. I was suddenly stagestruck, and losing my official aplomb, I gushed: "Well yes, Mr Borge! This is the Benson Hotel. I'll find you a piano right away, sir!" He smiled and thanked me, as I rushed off to locate one. "And perhaps an out of the way area to practice in?" he asked politely as I was heading down the corridor. "I'll do my best!" I called after him.

I stopped to use the house phone in the elevator lobby. There was always a grand piano on wheels in the Mayfair Room and I would have one of the housemen deliver it. Near my office was a service area, big enough to accommodate Mr. Borge and the grand piano he needed.

In just a few minutes two housemen could be seen pushing the concert grand towards us. It was maneuvered into the service area and Mr. Borge ran his hand over the polished surface. "Nice piano!" he said, seating himself and doing a test riff up and down the keys. "A little out of tune," he said, again smiling at me, "but it will do. I have to practice every day," he said, rubbing his hands together and stretching his fingers. "If I don't, I can tell the difference in my performance. Miss two days of practice and even my family can tell the difference. Three days and my audience can tell. What do you want to hear?" he asked and without waiting for an answer he started playing Chopsticks *"Do you know the tune?"* he asked with a smirk. I couldn't help but laugh and nod yes.

"Probably everyone knows Chopsticks!" he muttered good naturedly.

"I had lessons for ten years, when I was a kid."

"Did you, now? How far did you get?"

"Well, I was able to play *Clair de Lune* fairly well at a recital once."

"That's very good!"

After a moment, Borge seemed to forget I was there and in no time he lost himself in his practice. I was thrilled to hear this master pianist and felt I was privileged to have my own private concert. After sitting in a nearby chair and listening to him play for about twenty minutes I felt I was intruding on his private time. I stood up, offered a wave goodbye and he nodded in acknowledgement. Moments later I was in the fire exit and breathing the fresh air on SW Stark street.

Yeah, I thought to myself, this is a guy I'd pay to see, but not Bob Dylan, even if I did like his revenge song *Like a Rolling Stone* about the doomed rich girl Edie Sedgwick.

Taking on the Challenge of No Key Control

As I drove home, I thought about how the rich and famous (and the rich but not-so-famous guests) assumed they were in a safe environment when staying… *at the Benson of course.* Guests were, to a degree, safer from fire danger since the installation of several hundred smoke detectors in the rooms and since the establishment of the Emergency Response Team I had created.

However, the years of constant proliferation of guest room keys continued to be a serious danger and liability to the hotel. The truth was, absolutely no one knew how many *hundreds* of keys had been issued to a particular room and never returned. If only one tenth of one percent of those outstanding keys were in the hands of someone with ill intent, our guests were in danger.

The Connie Francis lawsuit had settled that issue even to Paul Mannerly's satisfaction. With Connie Francis in mind, I had studied the problem and considered the costs, and risks.

The best solution, and the most modern solution would be electronic key cards. The world's first optical electronic key card was introduced in 1979. The card reinvented hotel and motel room security and was first installed at the Westin Peachtree Plaza, in Atlanta, Georgia. The new key cards replaced old fashioned metal hotel room keys, which generally had the hotel name, address and room number listed, making it quite easy for people up to no good to prey on the unsuspecting. However, the cost to modify the doors in such a way, for the 287 rooms at the Benson Hotel would be prohibitive. I knew Paul Mannerly would never consider spending the necessary money on several hundred electronic key cards and what it would take to make them work by modifying the doors. It would have been a small fortune.

The next best solution was a compromise between cost and

guest safety but it would reduce the risk by at least a thousand percent. I decided on a (PAR) system, which means *periodic automatic replacement*, for guest room keys. After rekeying all the doors, only seven keys would exist for each room. The check-in desk would have four keys and my security office would hold the remaining three. When all seven keys had been issued but not returned, security would put the room "out of service" until the lock could be rekeyed, thereby ensuring guest safety and hotel security.

This was a compromise to be sure, but it meant a serious risk could be managed, and intelligently managed at that. With Paul Mannerly's approval, I signed a contract with a reputable Portland locksmith company and the task was begun. Needless to say, the front check-in desk clerks hated the new system. Now, they would have to ask the departing guest for their keys on check out and the front office key cabinet would look bare compared to the twenty or so keys they were used to having for each room.

Change riled everyone, but I was getting used to being vilified by the various dinosaurs of hospitality working at the Benson. I had spent almost 20 years being hated by criminals and other predators when I was a street cop and later a police detective. I had no problem being the Bad Guy, and couldn't have cared less what anyone thought of me. As long as I knew I was doing the right thing by maintaining safety measures at the Benson, I was content with my leadership style.

Contending With the Rampant Pillaging

During my lunch time conversations with Janet, who worked as our purchasing agent, she told me that Paul Mannerly was asking her why the costs were running so high? Food and beverage costs were too high, wine costs were too high, and linen costs were too high. Of course, I knew the reason for this—THEFT. Too much of the expensive sterling silver serving trays, coffee carafes, sugar bowls and the like were disappearing from room service trays, she told me. Replacement costs for the sterling ware were rapidly becoming prohibitive.

Mannerly was worried and upset, Janet said, and would ultimately have to explain to his father, the owner of the hotel, why costs were running rampant under his management. I decided a little snooping on my part would be in order. For several nights in a row I came to work on the graveyard shift and could immediately see part of the problem. Chef Bauser's kitchen was a convenient and generous sieve where a lot of groceries and foodstuff were disappearing into the hot hands of entitled employees who felt it was okay to steal.

In fairness to Chef Bauser, he was thrust into an impossible situation. He would often have to work until after ten in the evening at a fancy function and return at six in the morning to get breakfast up and running for the London Grill. I often wondered if he got more than about four or five hours of sleep each night.

Because of his endless duties, and out of necessity Bauser had his own room on the seventh floor, which was reserved for him exclusively. There he could catch as much rest as possible before starting the grind again. I don't know if Chef Bauser had a home, or a wife or a car because it seemed like he was *always* working and always at the Benson Hotel.

There was some jealousy of course among other department heads. Chef Bauser was the only employee who had his own room, but it was *necessary* and I understood that. In terms of the theft, whether the supply shrinkage was from his indifference or he simply didn't have time to think of everything, the high food costs at the Benson were becoming unsustainable. It became clear there was no system in place where locking up food was possible. So, because there was no way to lock up "the groceries," as Bauser called them, food continued disappearing.

On one of my late night inspections I found the only thing locked up in the kitchen were the walk-in coolers. In the bakery area, I found over one hundred pounds of sugar routinely unlocked in the sugar bin. The same for hundreds of pounds of baking flour unlocked in the flour bin. Five pound boxes of spices went missing from the bakery, especially cinnamon and particularly during canning season.

The ice cream freezer that served the London Grill and Room Service was unlocked and according to Janet, too often three gallon containers of ice cream just routinely disappeared. *Peppermint* was a favorite, and regularly low in stock. I found unused and unopened bottles of expensive wine sitting out, forgotten by tired employees, busy counting their tips and checking out. I could certainly see how being exhausted from work and long hours in a hot kitchen contributed to the losses, *and* the drinking.

I also knew how *easily* I could solve the problem.

I purchased several padlocks and hasps at the local Stadium Fred Meyer, and the next night I personally installed locks on unlocked bins and cupboards and on the ice cream freezer. The keys used to gain access to these areas would be checked out at security in the morning and returned to security at end of shift.

Another set of workable security measures created by this "rule crazy cop."

Naturally, Chef Bauser was furious when he could not initially access "the groceries" the next morning and clog-footed his way up to my second floor office for the key. "Vat's goinck on?!" he barked, glowering at me with his best and most severe expression of livid disapproval. "Vhy is everting locked up?" It took me about three minutes to explain to Bauser how things would be changing and that it was again "hotel security" that made these new changes necessary, because of the rampant theft going on in the kitchen.

After our short discussion, I took the opportunity to inform Bauser that I would need to take his photograph. He was not pleased. I then took the Chef's photo and issued him the very first key control card. Of course, Bauser was not happy about being the first to have a key control card but what else was new? Bauser was always disgruntled about something and considering his endless responsibilities, I couldn't blame him.

For those who might not understand, a "key control card" was not a *key card* but was rather a way for me to ensure all keys could be accounted for and would not go missing as a matter of course. The key control card was a laminated card with the department head's photo—the person authorized to be in possession of the keys and the key itself. This way, I knew where the keys *were* and *who* had them.

Again, Bauser was disgusted and angry that I was changing the way things had always been done *and* that his photo had to be taken. I will never forget how his mustache twitched as I tried to focus the camera, or the angry look on his face. I knew he knew I was amused and finding it hard to keep a straight face. I found that biting the inside of my cheek and hiding my face behind the camera helped in not breaking out in stifled laughter.

There was something so humorous about Chef Bauser's constant angst. It seemed he was always in a foul temper and on that we could rely. After dealing with him for so many years, it simply became funny to me. Though I always respected him for his expertise as a highly trained, gifted and creative chef who made the Benson the special place that it was, his constant grumpiness was amusing.

All department heads, Catering, Chefs, Sales Department, Purchasing, Housekeeping, Maintenance Engineers, Painters, and those who worked at Trader Vic's—anyone that carried master keys to *any* room were issued laminated key control cards with their photos. None of them were happy about it. Either the keys would be on their proper hook in my security office or the photo card of the person checking them out would be on the hook showing me exactly who had the keys and how long they had had them in their possession.

No more master keys would be allowed to "go home," or leave the hotel overnight ever again.

Now, absolutely *everyone* was mad at me except Janet in purchasing and several others who knew I was making the Benson safe and that I was an asset to the hotel. When I came up against opposition, I would shrug my shoulders, and evade responsibility by explaining it was "my job" and I had no choice but to do what was expected of me.

Many of the department heads and other employees seemed to take it as a personal affront that I tried to improve not only efficiency at the hotel but also safety. To them it seemed that the large ring of important looking keys they carried around with them all day and took home with them at night was their badge of authority. The more keys tinkling on the ring, the more important their personage, apparently.

Of course I relished the increased control I now had because I knew that overhead costs would go down. Costs going down would make my stature go up in the eyes of management. I was after all a department head too, but truth be told, I was beginning to tire of the denigrating stares I received or the way I was referred to as *"that security guy"* who came along and changed the way things had always been done.

Mushrooms? Why, of Course!

Why was I the only employee who genuinely worried about protecting the reputation of the Benson? Other department heads didn't seem to care as much, but I was aware of a whole host of possible disasters and I tried my best to manage those risks.

I often felt alone in that battle.

For example, the purchase of Bauser's blackmarket mushrooms, which had probably gone on for years was something I had to put a stop to, in order to protect the Benson from a possible catastrophe and the embarrassment of a televised scandal on every news station. In my mind's eye I saw the headline of the Oregonian Newspaper: *"Elderly European woman, a diplomat traveling from France, dies after being poisoned by tainted mushrooms served in a cream sauce. Benson Hotel Chef is currently being interrogated by police."*

As I'd had a history of dealing with another chef with questionable purchasing practices—Horst Mager, of the Rhinelander restaurant, back in the early 1970s when I was a detective with the Portland Police Bureau, I was more than familiar with the ways chefs regularly bought stolen seafood and other items off the street, via the blackmarket. Apparently, this included mushrooms! (Kennedy, 2022).

One afternoon, as I was doing my rounds, I found myself standing in the basement near the room service area. I was watching the goings-on in the kitchen, making sure no theft was occuring, and that the kitchen workers *knew* I was watching — which is an important element of running a successful business.

The stairway up to the Oak Street exit was just behind me and was the official fire escape route from the kitchen. While standing around for a few moments, I heard someone coming down the stairs from Oak Street. It was a scruffy, unkempt looking middle-aged man, and he was carrying a beat up, soggy cardboard box filled to overflowing with fresh, soil covered mushrooms.

"Where'd you get those?!" I asked the man pointedly.

"Oh, uh, here and there. In the woods mostly, I guess," he answered with a stricken look on his face. I saw him glance at my suit and nametag and read his mind as he figured out who I was and that I was someone of authority.

I leaned into him, and surveyed the contents of the box more closely, noticing the different variety of mushrooms. As I poked through them, I decided then and there we were *not* going to buy mushrooms out of a damp falling apart cardboard box, brought in by some scruffy, transient appearing person from the rain slicked streets of Portland, Oregon!

Just then, as I stood there, I heard the unmistakable sound of Chef Bauser, and his clippity-clopping wooden clogs, coming up behind me. I glanced back at him and saw he had a few dollars clutched in his hands, with the bills covered in a careless dusting of baking flour. Bauser gave me his usual look of hateful annoyance that again I was causing problems for him and sticking my nose into matters he must have felt did *not* involve me. Bauser extended his hand to the man, the bills in his hand, at the same time watching me with a stern look on his face, trying to gauge what I might do. The man clearly wanted the money, but he hesitated and waited for my response.

"You can't buy those, Xavier! You *can't* buy mushrooms off the street!" Bauser snorted a response and looked down, his ears red, his face contorted in fury. But I was furious, too.

"You'll get someone poisoned one day! Get the mushrooms from the regular distributor, for Christ's Sake!" Bauser remained angry as he glowered at me and his face continued to turn pink. His answer was unintelligible, as he was sputtering into his mustache, but it was clear he understood that while I was around *those* mushrooms would not be served at the Benson.

I had no doubt Bauser would do exactly what he wanted the minute I was not around. However, while I was doing my rounds, and in charge he would *not* buy blackmarket mushrooms off the street from some guy who looked like an old drunk trying to get enough money for a Mickey of Tokay—those cheap bottles of wine favored by Portland's local winos.

Nope! Not while *I* was around.

Since I had been appointed to the *Safety Committee* a few months before, I made it my business to nose around the entire hotel, and this included the kitchen. This irritated Bauser no end, especially when I would stand near the kitchen entrance and watch what was going on, my inscrutable poker face nonplussed at his or anyone else's annoyance.

What was referred to as "command presence" was something I learned to project as a police officer and detective. It came from years of having to be the *adult* in a lot of crazy situations with childish people and being called out to solve one dumb dispute after another. There were times when I felt I acted in the role of a parent to a lot of people who chose to behave like children.

Command presence became useful as a police officer, on more than one occasion to end silly disputes and family beefs between combative lovers, family members fighting over furniture after their parents died, drunk motorists and even tourists getting rolled for their wallets. Having that ability to take charge was useful while I worked at the Benson, particularly when I regularly had to escort out street people trying to pick pockets, walk off with leather purses or aggressively beg. It also came in handy when I had to set the kitchen staff straight about no more theft being allowed, and why.

To me my assertive attitude came naturally, but to others, they thought I was pushy, and bossy, and the mushroom confrontation exemplified that dynamic.

I realized Bauser was probably a master at hunting mushrooms and knew all the different species but I also knew there was always a chance something could get into the mix, like perhaps the Death Cap, (Amanita Phalloides) or the Destroying Angel, (Amanita Verna). Did the Benson want the *liability* in a lawsuit if Bauser was the source of the illicit mushroom collection? Wouldn't it be better if we could point the finger at someone else, such as a store we had purchased the mushrooms from?

My mother Clara DuPay, had been an expert mushroom hunter herself, and had belonged to the *Oregon Mycological Society*. She would drag me with her on her mushroom hunting expeditions when I was a teenager in the early 1950s, something I disliked because it meant being out in the wind and the rain, and getting muddy shoes. She told me tragic stories about how sometimes the Death Cap or Destroying Angel could get mixed in with other beneficial mushrooms, and all it took was *one* small Death Cap to destroy your liver and kill you, dead.

Her stories were never forgotten by me. All it took was one.

As Bauser walked away from me, furious and muttering under his breath, I wondered if he had the sense of a three-year-old.

All it would have taken was *one* single mistake and someone could wind up dead. As long as I was around, Bauser would buy mushrooms from legitimate sources and not off the street from blackmarket winos in dirty britches and muddy boots.

What is Accountability in Hotel Management?

I already had a good idea why the expensive silver serving ware, embossed with the Benson's name kept disappearing. On my routine walks of all the guest room corridors I couldn't help but notice room service trays dumped in front of occupied rooms. Guests would finish eating their room service meals and then push the tray out the door to be picked up by the room service attendants. Except they rarely got picked up in a timely manner. I often saw breakfast trays still parked in the corridors well into the evening meal.

This *invited* theft from all angles. Years later, in the 1990's, while garage sale hunting I found a serving tray from the Benson Hotel. I bought it and returned it to to the hotel. I explained I found it at a garage sale in S.E. Portland. The front office em-plyeee was surprised I had gone through the trouble.

No wonder the shiny, heavy-duty beautifully embossed silver was disappearing regularly. It was available to souvenir hunters for hours at a time, for both guests of the hotel and employees.

I found it distasteful having to tell the room service manag-er, Huong, how to do his job. However, my job, among other things, was to cut down on the theft of silver. It was *his* job to see that room service trays didn't sit in the corridors for hours on end. One memorable afternoon I waited until Huong turned in his master keys to my office. He was ready to go home, but I asked to speak with him.

He was in a hurry to leave, so I walked around him and shut my office door. Huong was surprisingly short, but an affable fellow who was part Asian and part Mexican with straight black hair that was always gleaming with Brilliantine hair oil. I encouraged him to sit on the edge of my desk while we chatted, because there were no other chairs in my office. After he hopped up, his feet didn't touch the floor, and while he had worked for many hotels, this was his first manager's position, which I knew made him feel proud.

I explained that Mr. Mannerly was "extremely upset" that so much expensive silver was disappearing and he felt it was Huong's fault. Without saying so directly, (because I didn't have the authority to fire him) I intimated that if he wanted to keep his job, the room service trays would now need to be picked up in a timely manner.

I let him know the Benson would not tolerate wholesale losses of embossed sterling silverware because *he* couldn't figure out how to insure the employees he supervised picked up the room service trays before evening and returned them to the safety of the basement. *"Do your damned job, okay?"* I said quietly, with a smile. Walking to the door, I opened it so he could escape my presence.

"You do your job, and I'll do mine. How's that?"

"Okay, sir!"

Huong slid off my desk and when his feet hit the carpet, he turned and bowed, a formal gesture I didn't expect. Feeling a bit softer toward him, I patted his shoulder, smiled and said: "I'm sure things will improve, now. Thanks for hearing me out." He smiled in return and nodded his head.

Huong backed out the door smiling and promising things would be different, and disappeared down the corridor. In the end, my tactic worked beautifully. In my mind, I imagined Huong meeting with his underlings and blaming *them* for the crime of the missing silver. I could see *him* using the same tone I'd used, telling them if they valued *their* job, they'd better make sure the room service trays were picked up, quickly, to avoid more blatant theft.

That was how the chain of command worked because it was necessary to be firm. I didn't like to come down hard on anyone but there were times when there was no alternative. That is the nature of the game in the hotel and motel business.

The change after a few weeks was that room service trays were now removed from the corridors shortly after the guests were finished with them and the silver theft dropped dramatically, saving the hotel considerable money. It didn't take Janet long to notice the difference either and we high-fived in the kitchen corridor a couple of months later, smiling at each other, after a scheduled staff meeting had disclosed the dramatic drop in silver theft.

Janet was the only manager that loved the changes I made, because it meant less financial loss for the hotel and a more squared away operation *and* more appreciation for not only my work but hers as well. Janet was definitely one of my staunch defenders.

Getting Drunk & Dancing on Tables

There was another thing I couldn't help noticing while walking the guest room corridors on my daily rounds, which was of course, the Marijuana smoke. Sometimes just wafting in the air, sometimes seeping out from under a particular room door, in a steady green cloud. It was obvious that a significant percent of the traveling public smoked pot and enjoyed it in the privacy of their rooms while traveling. Not just the rock bands that stayed at the Benson, but just regular folks traveling through town for business or pleasure. Of course it was none of my business what went on behind closed doors and I chose to ignore the pot smoke I smelled on a regular basis.

I recall once when a United Airlines stewardess forgot her marijuana pipe when she checked out and requested we mail it to her which we did. I chuckled when I thought that stewardesses were really sometimes high-in-the-sky while on the job.

Only *once* did the use of marijuana cause a real problem during my tenure as Director of Security. Trader Vic's Polynesian restaurant was the Benson's other high class dining destination and a favorite after work hangout for a particularly wealthy Portland seafood restaurant owner, by the name of Bill McCormick. It seemed that the more successful Bill's restaurant became (McCormick's Fish House) the more money he spent on Trader Vic's famous Mai Tai cocktails.

On this occasion Mr. Successful was having a party for about ten of his employees in Vic's private dining area. The doors that were normally closed for dining privacy were open because of the heavy cigarette smoke filling the room. In my wanderings around the hotel that particular evening I had already noticed these guests were well into their cups. This included boisterous conversations, along with a lot of hooting and hollering spilling out beyond the boundaries of the dining area.

Danny Fong, Trader Vic's manager, called me on my radio, concerned that this party was getting out of control. "They're making too much noise, Don. It's gonna disturb the other guests. Can you do something?"

One of the ongoing difficulties serving the wealthy is the problem of telling them when they've had too much to drink and will not be served anymore. After Danny and I met in the hall, we began to discuss the dilemma in hushed tones. "How do I tell this fella, he can't have anymore to drink?" Danny asked me, exasperated. "Jeez Don, he's already spent over a thousand bucks tonight and they just ordered more wine!" I stood next to him, looking at the floor and didn't answer. This was a tough one and I didn't know exactly how to proceed.

Danny shrugged his shoulders and looked puzzled, looking to me to solve this new problem. Born in Honolulu, he was half Hawaiian and half Chinese and had worked for Trader Vic's for over ten years. Tonight he seemed lost, struggling between serving his guests and keeping the hotel out of trouble. "I tried to be polite about it, but he just brushed me aside, and now he's standing on top of a table singing and smoking a joint while waiting for the wine steward to show up with more wine!"

"Ah, crap!" I muttered. "He's smokin' a jay?"

"Yeah!"

One of the easiest ways for a hotel to lose their liquor license is to allow the guests to get staggering drunk and then introduce drugs into the mix. The Benson Hotel's liquor license was worth many thousands of dollars each day and could not be jeopardized by one wealthy drunk idiot who was also smoking a joint on a tabletop.

But I had to be tactful.

I entered the private room and stood watching for a short while, letting this collection of executive imbibers become aware of my presence. A couple of women in their late 30s were dancing and laughing wildly. I stood off to the side, standing tall and saying nothing. When the wine steward arrived I had him clear the empty bottles away and remove the dirty ashtrays in a manner that indicated the party was over.

Then I had Danny deliver the tab. To the collective credit of most of them, the guests realized too much fun was being had. They all worked at Bill's successful restaurant and bar, (McCormick's Fish House) located on Beaverton Hillsdale HWY, and were used to dealing with similar situations themselves.

I offered my hand to help the gentleman down from the table and at the same time leaned in to him, and whispered loud enough for him to hear: "You know you can't smoke pot in a bar, right? You're in serious danger of making a fool of yourself. Lemme help you down and see you and your guests get home safely, okay?"

For a moment Bill looked at my serious face and I could tell he was thinking about telling me to go to hell, or worse. I extended my hand again, changing my look from serious to friendly. With a simple incline of my head and a pleasant smile, showing white teeth, I was giving him a way out, without losing face. We were friends, my face seemed to say and he was doing me a favor by cooperating. Bill had decided that perhaps I was indeed keeping him from making a fool of himself and he allowed me to help him down, hopping to the floor like a buoyant teenager.

An unexpected cheer arose from Bill's well-oiled employees partly in appreciation of his impromptu tabletop speech about God only knows what, and his drunken dance, and partly I think, because he came down *without* making a scene. I joined in the applause smiling, laughing and clapping indulgently, while secretly wishing they'd all just get the hell out. After the party goers started to gather their coats, purses and hats, I motioned Danny to go with me into the hall. I insisted he see that all the guests either took cabs home or found rooms at the hotel.

"After all, Danny," I admonished, "it was *you* who allowed them all to get this drunk. So *you* have to make sure they don't get hurt. You *do* understand that *you* are now personally and legally *liable*?" Danny didn't seem to understand, and stood across from me looking confused, but I smiled and patted his shoulder.

I knew it would give him something to think about later when he worried about losing his job. It is something all alcohol servers need to think seriously about. As a traffic cop for three years with PPB, I investigated hundreds of drunk driving accidents, including a gruesome "triple fatal" and I knew fully the dangers of trying to drive home while drunk.

Over serving guests until they become intoxicated is a serious moral and legal issue for any hotel but particularly for a high-end hotel like the Benson. The main problem was that many of the hotel's clientèle had *money* and were not accustomed to hearing the word *no*. Sometimes however, they *had* to hear the word *no* and I was happy to be the person to do that if I could.

Waitresses, Drunken Guests & Hotel Liability

Our cocktail waitresses depended a great deal on receiving tips when drinks were served and the more alcohol guests consumed the better the tips, often added to their credit cards with a grandiose intoxicated flourish by the drunk customer. Besides, the waitresses thought that most of the guests had rooms booked in the hotel and would not be driving home. It boiled down to money for the cocktail waitresses, (who had hourly wages that were frankly not that great) or liability for the hotel. The liability part put the problem within my purview, and it had the potential to become a serious issue, but a problem that I was eager to solve.

One of our most flagrant over-servers was a drop-dead gorgeous woman in her early forties, a former airline stewardess with a beautiful hourglass figure, long slender legs that went all the way up, and a soft British accent. Her name was Charlotte and she had been serving drinks in the lobby lounge for several years. Her auburn hair, almost red, was always well coiffed, worn up on her head in a soft feminine pile, kept in place with Bobby Pins, with loose curling tendrils framing her face.

Cherry Red lipstick adorned Charlotte's perfect rosebud lips, and her alabaster face powder and eye makeup was always perfectly applied. She had her own clientèle, regulars who were traveling businessmen. They would arrive from the airport and look for her specifically. They would come to visit with her, and have a drink before checking into their rooms, asking: "Is Charlotte in tonight?"

Being a shameless flirt was second nature to Charlotte, but it served her well. I remember one evening as she served an older man with a pot belly, she leaned over so he could see her cleavage, handed him his drink, and then I heard her playfully say: "I have your room number!" as if she might actually pay him a visit after her shift was over. I knew full well Charlotte would never visit this old guy's room, but she would lead him on to get that larger tip.

Charlotte was a challenge for me. She was so pretty and charming and always smelled so feminine and enticing it was hard for me to tell her that a particular guest was too intoxicated to be served again. My tactic at first was to lean against the bar in the lobby lounge and nod with a disapproving expression on my face in the direction of the offender, who might be drinking too much. But Charlotte often ignored me, batting her eyelashes innocently and smiling while patting her apron, jingling the tip money with the crunch of paper currency included.

Nature has a few laws that can't be broken, like the law of gravity, the law of supply and demand and for my purposes here, the law of *averages* which is the most important one. If you keep doing something bad, something bad will eventually happen. It wasn't long before an *I-told-you-so* moment worked to correct the over serving problem I had with Charlotte.

One evening near Thanksgiving, in the middle 1980s, I slipped into the hotel main floor via the underground tunnel from the basement parking lot structure next door. It was after midnight and I wanted to see how the bar patrons were making out. Standing at the end of the lobby lounge bar was a well-dressed businessman, his tie loosened and clutching a full shot glass in his left hand and a "water back" in his right. As he lifted and downed the shot he wobbled on his feet, almost falling, letting go of the water glass to hang onto the bar. He waved at Charlotte, motioning for her to bring him another shot, but my stern and steady gaze in her direction said *no more to drink for this guy*, in no uncertain terms.

At that point, the businessman turned, wobbling badly on his legs and staggered across the lobby to the marble stairs leading to the mezzanine level restroom. He managed the first two stairs before collapsing face down on the cold, hard marble. I could hear the sickening thud of flesh and bone on the fine, hard surface. As I jogged towards him, I saw an amazing and nauseating amount of blood coming from his flattened nose and a fractured tooth sticking through his bottom lip.

I was instantly brought back to the many bloody scenes I'd been called on to settle as a street cop patrolling the NE Albina district during the violent and chaotic 1960s and 1970s. I immediately started to sweat remembering the old days.

By the time fire department paramedics arrived a small crowd had gathered, "oohing and ahhing" including Charlotte who was now frightened because she knew *she* was in trouble. Everyone wanted to know what had happened. *"Just an accident. Just an accident. There's nothing to see here,"* I repeated quietly, urging people to move along. I was reminded of all the times I'd used those very same words at traffic accidents, bar fights, or even murders on the streets with a dead body growing cold on the sidewalk, or an old wino crushed in the gutter by a city bus. The thought made me want to laugh. Life didn't change much, did it? (DuPay, 2016).

One well-oiled guest walking down the staircase, sardonically suggested the poor man had been "attacked by the staircase." The man chuckled his way back to his drink which was waiting for him at the bar as if he were the funniest comedian ever to grace a stage. I felt disgusted as I watched him walk away, smug at the sight of all that blood. Why didn't people have the decency to get drunk at home, like everyone else?

Charlotte was holding a bar towel in front of her mouth in disbelief. Her eyes were wide and she was scared. She knew this was going to be a problem, and the way I glowered at her said just that: *This is your fault!* my face and eyes told her in no uncertain terms.

Patched up by the paramedics the drunk guest was escorted up to his suite and left to sleep it off. With cotton gauze stuffed up his nose, and his fractured tooth pulled out of his lip and a butterfly bandage placed over the laceration, I prayed he wouldn't think about suing. Because a guest had been injured and the paramedics called, I would have to write an incident report.

I was not pleased. In fact, I was furious.

"Why did you let this guy get so damned drunk he could barely walk?!" I demanded, after I steered Charlotte aside to a private corner so we could talk. Still holding the towel to her face, her eyes tearing up slightly, she replied by saying: "He didn't seem that drunk to me?!" Her squeaky little girl voice told me she was indeed worried.

After looking at the man's bar tab I could see that Charlotte had been tipped fifty dollars, signed with a signature barely legible, and just before the man walked over to the marble staircase and passed out, no less. "What luck!" I said, staring at Charlotte through my frown and knitted eyebrows. "He signed on your tip just in time!" I added sarcastically.

"What are you gonna tell Paul?" she asked, fearful now of losing her job. "I'm going to tell him that you served this guest until he was too drunk to walk! That the guest passed out on his feet and smashed his face on the marble stairway. And that you got a big tip for your efforts. That about covers it, right?" Charlotte's striking beauty seemed to diminish as she began to mop her teary eyes with the bar towel, making me wonder what she really looked like without all that makeup and in her just-out-of-bed rumpled hairdo.

Why did Charlotte try so hard to look perfect? Was it just to make better tips from the male guests or was it an extreme vanity she had to satisfy, to cover up some insecurity? I found myself wondering what her real backstory was, this former airline stewardess with a British accent. I told her to punch out and go home. "You're definitely done for the evening," I said. And just to really bring home what she'd allowed to happen, I added, "You've done enough damage for one shift!"

I didn't want Charlotte to lose her job and I felt sorry for both Charlotte *and* the drunk man. I felt sorry for Charlotte because she supported herself and depended a great deal on the generosity of strangers, and she needed to work. And I felt sorry for the guy because I knew he would wake up in the morning and see himself in the mirror with a damaged nose, severely cut and bandaged lip and a chipped tooth. And he would know deep down that no matter how much he'd tipped the pretty Charlotte she would *never* meet him in his room after her shift.

The guy was like so many others. He was never going to "get lucky" with a girl like Charlotte. She *was* a shameless flirt, but steadfastly refused to get tangled up with the men she served at the Benson. As for the guy who had smashed up his face, I hoped he wouldn't have a business meeting the next day, or worse, have to meet his disappointed wife at the airport and explain and/or lie about his injuries.

The next day I arrived at the hotel to find a note on my desk. Paul wanted to see me. My incident report was ready, explaining exactly what had happened along with the story about the pot smoking and very intoxicated guests in Trader Vic's which we had dealt with previously. As I sat in his office, drinking a cup of Bauser's strong coffee, with the perfect amount of fresh cream, I explained to Paul that the hotel could no longer take such risks with their liquor license.

And for good measure I added: "Paul, ultimately *you* are the one personally responsible for injury to a guest if your staff get them drunk. We can only hope this guy doesn't sue." I had spoken to Paul about his personal liability under Oregon law before, but I think *this* time it finally sank in as he clearly looked uncomfortable at the prospect of being sued by an injured guest because of the over-serving of alcohol.

"What should we do then, Don?" Paul asked, worried. "Do you think this guy with the broken nose is gonna give us trouble?" Paul shifted in his seat. He was definitely uncomfortable. "Well, I think the poor guy is too embarrassed to say or do anything," I replied. "But from now on the interests of the hotel must take priority over the interests of the servers. Even servers like Charlotte. Servers are just trying to make better tips by getting folks to drink, I understand that but *this* can't continue."

"I know, Don, I know."

"Paul, If you knew how many bars and taverns I got shut down for doing this very thing during the 1960s when I was a cop, and what the consequences can be—a month to two month's closure? Well, you might believe me when I tell you this *cannot* continue."

"Yes, I know it's important we curb this so that…" Paul's voice trailed off.

"Servers should *not* make the final decision whether to serve just one more drink. That decision has to be made by me, when I'm around, *and* the on duty bartenders. You know I was a cop for almost 20 years. I'm an expert on who's gonna be too intoxicated and who can *handle* another drink. And I have *no* problem being the bad guy here, no problem at all."

Paul shuffled around in his leather chair and then leaned back with both hands behind his head in thought. Just when I thought I'd have to prompt him again, he suddenly leaned forward, a smile on his face and a sigh of relief. "Go ahead and write the policy, Don! I'll sign it today. Security and the bartenders will make the final decision on when to stop serving alcohol to a guest."

I nodded my head in approval, glad he had not put up a fight. We both agreed the food and beverage managers would likely not be happy about this new change, as they would see it as just one more watering down of their authority by me, the hated Director of Security. But Paul and I also understood it was not their liquor license that was at stake. It was the *hotel's* liquor license, which constituted a substantial source of yearly revenue.

As I left his office, Paul sighed knowing he had made the right decision, with my help. I knew it was the right decision, too. I liked to see the boss happy. In just a few short months the controls via the policy changes I had made were showing very good results. Janet in purchasing was telling me she was having to buy less baking goods for the bakery and that was saving the hotel money. She was buying far less sugar, flour, ice cream, less wine, less silverware and less linen for the Housekeeping Department. Things were looking up.

In short my controls were acting like a tourniquet slowing the financial hemorrhaging that had been draining profit at the Benson Hotel for years. Things were tighter, locks were in place where they needed to be, keys were no longer going home with the housemen or the maids, room service sterling silver was being picked up when the guests were finished eating and expenses were coming under control. And I knew my reputation was improving. This became crystal clear with the other department heads when I was finally invited to join "the club."

A Severed THUMB?

One afternoon, as I was surveying the front lounge area, near the front entrance, I got a call on my Motorola radio from the PBX operator Marty, regarding a medical emergency on the top floor. She told me to get up there in a hurry, something about someone having cut their hand. On the top floor, we had a carpenter's shop. This was where licensed carpenters would fix dressers, chairs, and tables and anything else that needed to be repaired. They also did a lot of painting all throughout the hotel.

I took the elevator up to the 12th floor, and sprinted into the carpenters shop. There, I saw Ross, a longtime employee with the Benson. He was screaming bloody murder, jumping up and down, and weeping with tears streaming down his face. Poor Ross was obviously in shock and didn't know what to do.

Ross had severed his left thumb on the table saw and blood was spurting everywhere. He had stuffed his hand into his dirty blue work apron, to stop the bleeding, but it wasn't working very well. The thumb had been cut off cleanly at the upper joint. I could see what had happened and even saw the severed thumb as it lay, forlornly, on the flat surface of the table saw, minus its owner spurting blood everywhere.

I ran down the hall, thinking to myself that this was not the day I had expected, but remembering that anything could happen at the Benson Hotel and regularly did. At the ice machine, near the front of the hall, I grabbed the large plastic ice scoop and filled it with ice. Then I sprinted back to Ross, with ice cubes falling left and right as I ran. Once back in the room, I grabbed a white towel, which was laying on the saw, and poured the ice into it. Then I carefully picked up the severed thumb, between two fingers, grabbed Ross's hand and stuffed both inside the ice filled towel, wrapping them up firmly.

I tried to console Ross as he wept, and told him, "The ambulance is on the way. You'll be alright." He was distraught, his face awash in tears and I felt terribly for him.

Because the PBX operator had called emergency services right away, it wasn't even one minute later that the elevator door burst open and the paramedics rushed in. They loaded Ross onto a gurney and we all took the elevator down to the first floor, where I watched as they rushed him out the front door and directly to the hospital. As I stood there, catching my breath, I realized I had blood on my hands. I trudged tiredly into the mens' restroom where I washed my hands and reflected for a few minutes on being Director of Security. What a thing to happen, I thought to myself.

Ross was off work for a few weeks, but his thumb was reattached, and he was able to return to work sometime later. Though his thumb would never work the same, and had limited mobility, at least he didn't lose it. The experience was traumatizing. I felt very sad for Ross and again wondered why it was that I seemed destined to see so much blood in my life.

Weekend "Duty Officer" was a Step in the Right Direction

Hotel policy dictated that a member of management, a department head, be in charge of the hotel on weekends to exert a visible "management presence" and to partake of all the services available and write a report to be turned in to Paul on the following Monday. The job of "weekend duty officer" was passed around evenly—each department head taking their turn.

It would be my turn about once every six weeks. Any hesitation about "that security guy," looking over the restaurant service on weekends finally dissolved when they realized that I was more than just some dumb gumshoe ex-cop, unqualified for work in the hospitality industry.

I had been raised in the restaurant business, something I let them all know over time, having worked for years in my parents' successful restaurant, *DuPay's Drive-in Restaurant*, which was in business all during the prosperous and innocent 1950s. Moreover, I had two years at Lewis and Clark college under my belt, having attended right after graduating from Grant High School in 1954 as an honor student. I had more than enough "food and beverage" experience coupled with an understanding of how restaurants were managed, cleaned *and* made safe from burglary and robbery.

I had come to the Benson Hotel *made* for the job of Director of Security.

"Weekend duty officer," was a club I was eager to join. It allowed me to check into the hotel after four in the afternoon on Friday, pick up my evaluation packet, choose just about any room I wanted, order room service hors d'oeuvres and a glass of champagne and sit with my feet propped up watching TV until I was hungry and ready for a sumptuous Benson Hotel dinner.

While sitting and sipping my champagne I would fill out the evaluation page for Housekeeping, checking to see if the bed was made properly, and the carpet vacuumed correctly. I further had to make sure that the smoke detector worked *with* batteries, and that there were no stray pubic hairs left in the bathroom shower stall or behind the bathroom door. The room service menu had to be present, along with a Gideon Bible in the drawer of one of the night stands, and the clock set for the proper time. It all had to be in place.

When I finished snacking, I placed my room service tray outside the door and informed the front desk I was finished eating. They would inform the kitchen that I was done, and I knew the room service kids would be timed on how long it took them to retrieve the silver service tray from the corridor floor, to prevent the theft of its component parts.

Once room service had completed their task I filled out their portion of the evaluation sheet. If there were no hotel problems to deal with, I decided I could postpone those issues and watch the local news until dinnertime. At about eight in the evening, a fashionable time for my dinner entrance, I would dress, making sure my black three piece suit, dress shirt and tie looked perfect. I would comb my hair and splash some Old Spice aftershave on my face and neck. I made sure the black and gold name badge with my name and position was properly showing on my lapel, and would take the elevator to the mezzanine. From the mezzanine I could look down over the entire lobby, making sure all was in order.

I would then make my entrance down the elegant polished marble stairway, pausing to smile at the beautiful harpist, a lovely young woman with long, pale ash-blonde hair. She regularly played classical music on the landing and her image was reflected in the grand palace mirror secured to the wall. The giant silver plate mirror was handcrafted, made in Paris in 1883 for a castle in Hawaii, and purchased to grace the lobby of the Benson Hotel sometime in 1958. With my hair slicked back and my impeccable black suit on, I felt a little like Rhett Butler coming down the grand staircase in the 1939 film, *Gone With The Wind.*

I enjoyed the obvious theater of my grand entrance. It was to let everyone know that the Security Director, Don DuPay, the new weekend duty officer, or as some of the staff still called me, "that security guy" was in charge and in the house. It was fun walking down the grand staircase. Now, all I had to do was saunter over to the lobby lounge, walking slowly, looking about me, taking time to be seen by all the employees, and order another drink before deciding on *which* elegant restaurant I would dine in that evening.

I recall my first Friday evening, as the weekend duty officer. The crowd in the lobby lounge were all happily drinking expensive spirits and eating hors d'oeuvres from laden trays from either the London Grill or Trader Vic's. They were clearly enjoying the quiet and serene music coming from the pretty blond harpist who exuded class and understated sophistication—a perfect addition to the Benson.

I ordered a Manhattan, heavy on the Vermouth, with two olives, from Charlotte (who was still with us) and watched her move smoothly in and out of the crowd. She drifted by, serpentine fashion, serving drinks, and smiling brightly, batting her eyes and making promises to the men she would never keep. Charlotte was smooth, a pleasure to watch while I sipped my drink, and smelled her lovely department store perfume as she sashayed around.

But it was a different Charlotte. She was trying hard to obey the rules and I found her occasionally glancing at me and nodding imperceptibly at a particular patron, asking for my assurance that it was still okay to serve the person, usually a man, yet another drink. We communicated in a large room with nonverbal cues and no one was the wiser. When I saw a man who was not drunk, I barely nodded my head in her direction, giving her the go ahead, and she nodded back.

Things were going well at the lobby lounge that Friday evening. The Benson was at its most elegant, conservative best and my evaluation would reflect that. That night I would dine in the London Grill and as nine o'clock approached, I crossed the lobby again and proceeded down the carpeted stairway to the lower level restaurant.

The young handsome *maître d'* greeted me and gestured with his arm, indicating I could choose the table I wanted. I decided on a back table, the one where I'd seen Moshe Dayan and his armed guards eating from, as it allowed a view of the entire dining area. I would sit with my back to the wall, a common habit among former and retired law enforcement. I ordered coffee with my dinner of prime rib and Bauser's perfect whipped mashed potatoes, tossed green salad and simmered vegetable medley, and settled back to enjoy my dinner and watch the goings on from a discreet distance.

The London Grill was packed with the wealthy that night, enjoying quality wine elegantly served by the knowledgeable wine steward, and the finest steak, prime rib and Cornish game hens. All the servers were male waiters formally dressed in tuxedos, complete with the obligatory white towel draped over their left arm. The ambient music seemed to come from nowhere and blended in with the hushed conversations of those dining. This was a fancy place and I felt both humbled and lucky to dine there. And all I had to do was sign the check. It was free!

My dinner and the service were impeccable. Of course they knew they were serving the "weekend duty officer" and would be graded on their performance. That evening I would give them a superior grade on both food and service and I sat for a moment sipping a second cup of rich dark coffee while filling out the London Grill evaluation form and finishing the last of my salad. Paul Mannerly expected at least a grade of "above average" to "superior" on the food service, and all the employees knew this, but the crew there were all seasoned professionals and they knew they worked at the best joint in town!

After finishing my late dinner, I made an appearance at Trader Vic's, standing unobtrusively near the dining room where the drunken restaurant owner, Bill McCormick, and marijuana orator had held forth, dancing on the tabletop only a few days before. I was pleased at how this sumptuous and equally elegant restaurant was operating. I would dine at Trader Vic's on Saturday evening, the following night, but for now walking around the hotel with the evening atmosphere of soft music, the savory aroma of well made food and the sounds of tinkling beverage glasses, I could just as easily have been in a beautiful European palace.

I took it all in. The ceiling was alabaster white and patterned with many ornate ceiling medallions, highlighted with shimmering gold paint. It exuded the aura of a cathedral and rivaled the elegance of Versailles, befitting the equally elegant Austrian crystal chandeliers and seemed to possess a slightly French Rococo-like elegance.

After dinner, I stopped to chat with the check-in counter girl, and learned that both Merv Griffin and Ed McMahon would be checking in, and would be taping a TV show in the lobby in the morning. I believe this coincided with Merv Griffin visiting Portland in 1982, for the Grand Floral Rose Festival Parade, where he would be acting as the Grand Marshall. Two more celebrities I would get to see! But for now I stopped again at the lobby lounge and ordered a Grand Marnier. It was my favorite liqueur and would top off my evening perfectly, before heading to bed, where I would pass out on one of the comfortable king size beds.

My room that night was on the second floor, at the southeast corner of the hotel, Suite 209, and overlooked downtown Broadway Street. It was the closest room to the fire escape and being on the second floor, in the event of a catastrophic fire, the fire department could rescue me if necessary. No taking chances for me, I thought to myself as I undressed for bed.

The smoke detector was working and with three extra pillows to snuggle, I drifted into an uneasy sleep. The specter of some awful emergency I would have to solve hung in my mind, as it sometimes did when I tried to sleep. I had regular nightmares about my days as a Portland police officer and all the chaos and bloody scenes I'd witnessed after being called in to resolve one problem after another.

At 2:35 A.M. I awoke suddenly realizing I was not home. I opened the window far enough to stick my head out. It was misting and the street below was dark because of it and slick looking. The air smelled of wet pavement and muffled the noise of the few cars still downtown that late. It was like standing in the future and looking down at my past, gazing down at that wet street. How many times had I cruised Broadway street at night as a teenager showing off my shiny 1946 Plymouth, in the early 1950s, or parking in front of the Jolly Joan Restaurant for a milkshake, hoping to meet a pretty girl?

And how many hundreds of times had I driven up Broadway as a patrol cop, working out of Central precinct? A lot of my life had passed on that slick street down below. But now my life was above the street and I was in charge of security for the finest luxury hotel in the city of Portland, just as I had once been in charge of the myriad streets below as a young police officer. I left the window open and returned to bed, and curled into the hotel's standard pink sheets. If I could drift back to sleep, I might be able to get enough rest until I had to get up again.

At 6:30 A.M. I awakened and being in a strange bed I wondered again where I was. Oh yeah, I was *working*. I rubbed my eyes and reached for the bedside phone. Wiggling around the pink pillows to reach it, I dialed room service and they answered on the second ring, knowing that it must be the weekend duty officer calling.

"Send up a pot of coffee, some cream and two butter croissants, please," I said politely. I loved Chef Bausers perfectly cooked butter croissants. The man was an artist and a genius at cooking and baking. There was simply no one better. The food Bauser made, whether savory or sweet, was a kind of magical confection, so as to melt in your mouth. His butter croissants were light and fluffy and gently dissolved in your mouth the way good champagne kind of fizzes in your mouth, like sweet fog when you drink it.

No one could make soft buttery croissants like Chef Xaiver Bauser, that's all I knew and I was looking forward to them.

It took room service ten minutes to deliver my order. After I opened the door, the elegant sterling silver tray and silver coffee pot were placed on the table by the room service attendant, who left discreetly, not waiting for or expecting a tip. I opened the curtains to see an already busy downtown street bustling with activity. The traffic sounds came through the open window with the smell of fresh misty Portland air. The coffee was perfect and so were the croissants. This small repast would hold me until I could have breakfast at the Grill in the next hour.

After eating, I shaved and then jumped in the shower, soaping myself up and washing my hair. The bathroom was elegant with mirrors on the walls and a floor of tan tiles with bright white grout. The towels were heavy, soft and elegant, if towels *can* be elegant, but these towels were. They had fine stitching and no razzles or torn threads, and they felt great on my wet skin. Soon I was dressed and ready to go. I took the elevator down to the mezzanine, a favorite hangout, as it was a kind of tower from which I could view the lobby without being seen by employees or guests.

Preparations for the taping of the Merv Griffin special were already underway. Three cameras were being positioned, and lighting was being arranged. One of our building maintenance men was furnishing extra power cords to get everything plugged in properly. Merv and his co-hosts sat in luxurious brown leather easy chairs and three makeup people were dabbing at their faces with makeup pads, smoothing down their hair with combs, and spraying hairspray.

One of the Bellmen held a sign that read: "Quiet please! Taping in progress!" and the show began filming. I made my way down the grand stairway and ordered my breakfast to be sent to the Lobby Lounge, where I ate and watched the celebrities chat and interact. I have no idea what the show was about except I believe it was a benefit for a children's charity. Guests that were lucky enough to be checking in were impressed by the presence of Merv Griffin hanging out in the lobby with his entourage of show employees.

It made the Benson even more renowned. I wondered if I should pinch myself to see if this was all real and smiled to myself as I stood there, watching. The rest of my day was spent roaming the hotel, being seen and talking to employees, making sure everything was running smoothly. I spent several hours in my office studying recent hotel liability newsletters, considering the changes to the laws and drinking coffee. It was my job to know what the courts were requiring of hotels and to stay abreast of all changes to hotel liability law. In this way, I could learn how those laws might impact the Benson Hotel.

I skipped lunch in the employee cafeteria, stopping in for a minute to say hello to some of the workers and then I went back to my room where I took off my shoes, laid on the bed, punched up all the pillows and fell asleep. Being in charge of hotel security, and a general overseer if you will, might have seemed like a cake job but the stress of being-in-charge was always there. In a way, it reminded me of the stress of managing a crime scene when I was a detective and making sure vital evidence was not destroyed by a young inexperienced patrolman touching, or walking all over things and mucking things up.

I woke up a couple hours later, got up, brushed my teeth and dressed in my black three piece, and got ready for my upcoming evening of eating and drinking well. But it was still an hour or two before I would put in my official appearance.

Looking Down at the City of Portland

Bored, I went up to the roof for some fresh air and a view of the city. It had cleared after a night of drizzling rain and I could see as far as Mt. Hood in the east. The view was so great I sometimes wondered why we didn't have a small elegant rooftop bar—just then housekeeping, one floor down, turned on all of the large dryers at once. The vibrations and constant shaking made me wonder about the integrity of the entire structure. I wondered how many years of shaking the building it would take before it all collapsed in a dusty implosion. I should talk to the fire marshal about it, I mused to myself, making a mental note to inquire about how quake proof the building actually was.

Inspecting the entire roof took me a short while, pausing to look over the edge, all those stories below and checking behind air conditioning vents for employee contraband. This included such things as purloined bottles of wine, cigarette butts and used condoms, as I had found before upon occasion. Luckily for the employees, I found nothing on that day.

Taking my last deep breath of pristine fresh air, I ducked into the doorway and walked down the stairwell to housekeeping, where I shouted hello to the Executive Housekeeper. She was a thin dark haired woman and as tall as my six feet. The huge row of dryers made the laundry area humid and she had beads of fine perspiration on her brow. It was hot and noisy and the constant "whump-thack" of the linen folding machine made it hard to hear anything. I nodded, and she smiled pleasantly as I turned to leave, happily making my way to a more elegant, air conditioned section of the hotel.

I took the service elevator straight down to the mezzanine where I could overlook the lobby and assess the goings-on before heading down the marble stairs. I stopped to say hello to the check-in clerks and the on-duty bellmen, whom I could tell were trying to present a more personable and professional image. Employees that usually saw me as only "that security guy," were now beginning to understand that I had an important job to do and they seemed to respect me more.

I ordered a glass of red house wine at the lounge and sat where I could view the entire lobby, with my back to the wall, naturally. The Benson's house wine was a Pinot Noir variety from the Willamette Valley's *Sokol Blosser* winery, which had been founded in 1971. Our wine steward assured me that Sokol Blosser was a man's name (he was wrong) and that they made "quality Oregon wine" fit to be served at the Benson. Well, he was right about *that*. I discovered years later that the name was actually a meshing of the married couple, Susan Sokol and Bill Blosser's last names, and their wine was indeed excellent and remains excellent to this day.

I nursed the glass of wine over the course of an hour and watched Tracy Barry, a local TV news anchor, sit and order her own after-work drink. She sat with an attractive young gentleman and they seemed subdued and perhaps even tired as they sipped their drinks. She was the cuddly, blond, cute, girl-next-door type, and presented a believable image on our local news when she delivered the news in her competent laid back style.

Laurie the "Unwanted" Deserved an Oscar!

My wine drinking and girl gazing was interrupted, at that point, by the surreptitious entry through the Oak Street side-door of *Laurie*. Laurie was a well-known "unwanted," a persona non grata, a beggar/alcoholic who rarely bathed. But Laurie was different from the routine drunks and shabbies who constantly wandered into the hotel begging for money for a bottle of gut rot booze. Laurie was a professional beggar, and quite good at what she did. Her act began as she furrowed her brow, squinting her eyes, looking both left and right, and seeking the next potential victim. They would be sitting unaware in our lounge, immersed in their cocoon of drinks and conversation, and then she would suddenly appear out of nowhere.

Spotting a likely pushover, Laurie would lumber in their direction as a 260 pound sack of lumpy potatoes might be seen lumbering, *if* it could walk. Her steps were deliberate and measured, with an awkward gait. She lifted up the back of her heels in an abnormal way which demonstrated the years of late stage alcoholism and brain damage which had morphed into what police sometimes called "the drunk walk." Her once white tennis shoes could barely be seen below the layers of filth that clung to them. Dirty sweaters, jackets and thin coats were layered over equally dirty gray sweatpants. She appeared as if she was wearing her entire wardrobe at the same time.

As Laurie closed in on her victims personal space, her act began with the ringing of hands and real tears which streamed from her gray eyes. Yes, they were real, appearing as if by magic, as she whimpered her message of desperation. "Please sir, (or madam) I'm homeless and need money for rent and food."

Her messy strands of long hair escaped from a faded blue scarf she used as a hat, helping to frame her heavily jowled face. The striking resemblance Laurie bore to Hollywood actor Charles Laughton as he appeared in the 1939 movie, "The Hunchback of Notre Dame," was notable. Laurie could have *been* Charles Laughton in rags, doing drag, she bore that much of a resemblance to him.

Though she didn't quite recognize me at first, as I sat there with the rest of the customers drinking my wine, Laurie knew who I was. I stood up and began walking in her direction. Realizing I had spotted her con artist routine, the tears stopped immediately and her hands balled into fists of frustration, as her head went down. Laurie was furious now, as she knew the game was over.

Laurie did an "about face" and moved slowly back toward the Oak Street door. She turned around, looking over her shoulder hatefully, and furrowed her brow, and at a distance of about fifteen feet, she spat in my direction with a one-eyed squint. She waddled her way out the door. I couldn't hear what she said but I was sure it was something like: "I'll be back, you bastard! You won't catch me every time!" And I'm sure she was correct.

I apologized to the corpulent businessman in the blue Armani pinstripe, explaining that we did our best to keep the undesirables away and told him that the Benson would be happy to buy his next drink. He stood up to shake my hand, wiping his mouth with a white monogrammed handkerchief and accepted my offer. As the bartender delivered the man's drink, I returned to my empty wine glass and ordered a coffee with lots of cream.

Tracy Barry was still in the company of the preppy looking young man. He wore a black suit with a white tie and dressy red suspenders. They were crossing the lobby to have dinner at the London Grill. She was but one of many of the well-known locals and frequented the Benson for dinner and drinks regularly, and I was always happy to see her pretty face and beautiful blonde hair.

Mayor Frank Ivancie & the Driver

Another local celebrity who frequented the Benson Hotel was Portland mayor, Frank Ivancie. He visited the Benson's lobby lounge about three days a week, presumably after a hard day of politicking at city hall. The truth is, the mayor came for one reason and one reason only and that was to get drunk — at least that's what usually happened.

Mayor Ivancie was nicknamed "Ivancie The Terrible," by the local newspapers and news media for his draconian stance on hippie activists, low income families needing social services, and of course the gay and lesbian folks who made Portland their home. This is what I remember. The mayor thought the hippies should go back to California, and that the city had no business providing for or supporting social services for such people. He also openly spoke out against gays, hence the nickname, "Ivancie The Terrible."

Ivancie always arrived in the company and safety of his armed police driver in a city owned vehicle, and parked in the "fifteen minutes only" hotel zone until he was ready to leave, usually about 90 minutes later. His police driver was none other than

The Benson Hotel in the 80s. Photo courtesy of Scott Allen Tice.

the late Sergeant Mike Garvey, of the Portland Police Bureau. Garvey was handpicked to be Ivancie's driver, it was rumored, because Sergeant Garvey had class, was reserved, looked sharp in his suit and tie and came from an okay, middle-class family.

When I was on duty, I would often spend time chatting with Sergeant Garvey out in front, on the sidewalk, next to the front doors. Although we had never worked together as police officers, as he had come on many years after me, Garvey was well-known and well-liked, and I enjoyed our meandering conversations.

I felt sorry for Garvey as he often had to sit, drinking coffee in the lobby lounge, bored and twiddling his thumbs while waiting for the mayor to get drunk enough to go home. I never did tell the bartender to stop serving the mayor when he became drunk. He was an exception. Ivancie *was* after all the mayor of Portland, and was already in police custody, so to speak.

Sergeant Garvey would often assist Ivancie unobtrusively toward the front door when it was time to go, never letting him stumble and helping him into the car. Garvey generally had a sheepish grin on his face, as if he was babysitting a small child, when he escorted the mayor out. I could tell he was embarrassed. I nodded and smiled a sympathetic goodbye. Most cops don't like dealing with drunks, particularly drunk politicians and Garvey and I understood each other.

A few years after Mike's driving-the-mayor-around-town duties were over, Sergeant Garvey came out as a gay man. He was the *first* openly gay male police officer to serve in Portland. It just goes to show you, you can't always tell by looking, because Mike Garvey came off very straight. I never had a clue he was even the slightest bit gay. He had command presence and came off ultra masculine so it just never occurred to me that he might be gay. I remember him as being intelligient, friendly, and a great conversationalist.

Garvey must have gloated every day knowing he had fooled Frank Ivancie, who clearly never knew. I wonder if maybe Garvey hated Ivancie just a little bit for his ignorance and anti-gay stance. I have always felt it's no one's business what you do in your personal life, just as long as no basic laws are violated.

Mike Garvey passed away in August of 2020 at age 68 after a short battle with prostate cancer. He had just completed his dream home in Palm Springs. He left a lasting legacy of 28 years working for the Portland Police Bureau in which he helped many Portlanders and always fought for the underdog.

Entering the Fantasyland of Trader Vic's

After one glass of wine and two cups of coffee I was beginning to get hungry, and looking forward to my elegant dinner in Trader Vic's. Trader Vic's was always my all time *favorite* place to eat at the Benson. The Polynesian theme and the tiki atmosphere allowed the guests to enter another world, thousands of miles out in the tropical South Pacific. It reminded me of the times I'd spent in Honolulu when I was in the Navy Reserves in the 1970s and the Waikiki atmosphere that was lush, fun and seductive.

The doorway from the lobby into Trader Vic's was made to look like you were entering a large grass hut. The smell from the glass enclosed wood-fired Polynesian barbecue lured you in with the promise of delicious food. I was greeted by Danny the Honolulu born, Hawaiian and Chinese manager, dressed in a dark blue blazer and gray slacks. Danny's round face was topped off by jet black hair, slicked back, and perfectly coiffed. He smiled, the wide, sincere smile he reserved for VIP's, or week-end-duty officers such as myself, and directed me to a nice corner table where I could dine in privacy, yet view the entire restaurant.

Since I had rescued Danny from embarrassment while dealing with the drunken restaurant owner, Bill McCormick, who had been smoking a joint and standing atop a dining table, yelling, singing and acting like a court jester, Danny and I had become good friends.

Mai Tai's were "invented" at Trader Vic or so the legend goes, and so of course I had to order one. Sipping my drink and perusing the dinner menu, I selected the juicy barbecued pork and wild rice that was so popular. In the meantime I snacked from the tray of "pupu's" which included small egg rolls and fresh sushi, along with some Crab Rangoon, and Stuffed Shrimp.

I couldn't bring myself to eat raw-fish sushi however, and left it on the plate, untouched. Danny cleared away the pupu plate, shrugging, but smiling. I was sure the sushi would not go to waste as it was untouched and would soon disappear into the kitchen and into someone's grateful mouth.

Over my head, securely fastened to the bamboo thatched roof ceiling was a long outrigger canoe, with fishnet hanging from the sides as if it was left there by an actual fisherman. The subdued lighting came from netted glass floats turned into light fixtures. Each individual dining table was illuminated by a large white clam shell which was back-lighted by a soft gold bulb. Puffed up blowfish, varnished stiff and spiny also added to the tiki theme. Carved wooden tiki gods, four feet tall, were placed about the room, adding a somewhat fearsome look along with the crossed spears attached to the wall thatch. The décor was dark, mysterious, exotic and primitive all at the same time.

After I finished my meal I ordered a Kahlua and Crème which I sipped leisurely, while I filled out the rating questionnaire. They would get an exceptional rating that night, both in food and in service. I glanced at the total of over fifty dollars, added a fifteen percent tip, and signed the ticket. I loved belonging to the weekend duty officer's club. I loved being treated like a VIP. I loved the attention and again I felt lucky to work at the best hotel in town. Life was good, and getting better all the time.

When I had completed the questionnaire, I exited the front door of the Benson onto SW Broadway and Stark and walked around the entire block. I watched the street people and sniffed the crisp, fresh air. I entered the hotel again through the north facing, Oak Street side door. I was sleepy after my meal and drink, but I still had to walk around, being seen and talking to the employees, as that was an important part of the job. By eleven at night, I knew I should have a final drink at the lobby lounge, observing their operation before I could go and crash in my second floor suite and get a good night's sleep.

While I leaned against the end of the bar sipping my Grand Marnier, I made notes on the rating sheets for Paul Mannerly. This made the staff nervous, watching me write things down.

I 'theater-ed it up' a little, looking first at the bartender, then glancing down and writing something (or pretending to) and then looking pointedly at the cocktail waitress, then jotting down something more. I enjoyed messing with them, and it was pretty obvious that I was, but perhaps not to *them*. It kept them on their toes, having me watch them and catch their surreptitious, nervous glances in my direction.

Finally, I signed the drink ticket, put my gold Cross ballpoint pen in my breast pocket, folded up the rating sheets and walked to the elevators. I could feel the lounge staff heave a sigh of relief. They were glad I was gone for the night. And I was, too. It had been a long day.

The following morning was Sunday, and I was able to sleep past ten. There had been no emergencies, no kitchen fires, no assaults. The London Grill Sunday brunch was up and running and it would be my last inspection meal of the weekend duty.

Chef Bauser's brunch offering was impressive. Ham, bacon, and sausage, both link sausage, and patty, all high quality, and cooked to perfection, eggs poached or scrambled just like I liked them, mashed potatoes or hash browns and stacks of perfectly sized small hot cakes, along with a huge selection of fresh fruit. At the end of the line were the beverages, orange juice, grapefruit juice, coffee, a selection of English teas, milk and ice water from a large sparkling glass carafe filled with lemon and cucumber slices. I filled my plate and was escorted by a waiter to a corner table. They knew I was coming of course.

This would be my last free sumptuous dining experience for at least six weeks and I had stuffed myself accordingly. After finishing a double chocolate covered brownie, washed down with two more cups of dark hot coffee with lots of cream, I had to unbutton the top button of my suit pants. I signed the ticket, stuck it in my suit pocket and waddled back to the elevator lobby. My duty was over now and I was free to go home.

I could sleep the rest of the day in my own bed, in my own little apartment. I would be able to shed all vestiges of my official looking, black three-piece-suit. This included lounging around in my underwear, drinking beer, snacking on Cheetos and Corn Nuts, and watching television. Yes, life was good while working for the Benson Hotel.

Cheryl Falcone &
a Million Dollar Lawsuit

A particular Monday morning came, as relentlessly as Mondays always do, and when I arrived at the hotel there was a sticky-note on my office door. Paul wanted to see me immediately. I was curious what the issue was and wondered if perhaps I had slept through some new hotel emergency. I was ready for trouble when I knocked on the boss's door. "Come in Don!" I heard Paul call out. I opened the door to see a very upset Paul pacing back and forth behind his desk with a wrinkled letter clutched in his left hand.

"What is it boss?" I inquired, walking to a chair in front of his desk and sitting down. I couldn't help but wonder if someone had written a nasty letter about me, maybe a rich drunk I had cut off at the bar, or a disgruntled employee, fed up with my demands that they do their best and stop stealing from the kitchen.

"It's that Falcone woman! The woman who got beat up here? She's causing trouble. This letter is from our corporate attorneys in Seattle. We're being sued for over a million bucks, Don!"

He stopped pacing and read from the letter word for word. "Her attorneys are claiming that because we didn't provide *reasonable* care, she was beaten up in an attempted robbery, and because of our *negligence* she had to be hospitalized and has a permanent scar on her forehead. I can't believe this!"

I could tell that Paul was frightened as he handed me the letter and slumped into his leather chair. I took the letter and read it slowly, pausing to think over the events of when I first heard Cheryl Falcone screaming in front of her room on Nine South, while being pistol whipped.

I thought about the event, going over it point by point, in my mind. I had fortuitously been on the 9th floor patrolling the corridors, and was able to hear her screams, and I appeared in time to frighten off her assailant. My quick response kept her from being hit with the pistol a third time, which could have caused considerably more injuries. I had summoned immediate professional medical care and had comforted and questioned her until medics arrived and she was sent to the hospital. I contacted police and gave the officers a description of her assailant. As I remembered him, the description she provided to police had been entirely different.

What else could I have done? I knew that we had indeed provided reasonable care as the courts required of hotels and I told Paul this confidently. "It should be a slam dunk in our favor, Paul," I said, casually. "Don't worry about it. It's not gonna be as bad as you think." He looked across at me and I could see he was unconvinced.

I could well understand his concern. From his point of view, the Benson was being sued for over a million dollars. There could be no *good* publicity over this. The hotel's reputation might be damaged, and it had all happened when *he* was in charge as the General Manager.

I could tell that he was worried about what his father would think if we lost the lawsuit. "The trial starts next Wednesday at the King County courthouse in Seattle," he said. "At nine sharp. I've arranged for our rooms at the downtown Seattle Westin hotel. Gayle Patmon, the front office manager? She's the one who checked Falcone in, and Marty. She notified the police and ambulance, after you called her on your radio. They will both have to come and testify, too. Do you want to ride in my car with us?"

The prospect of being locked in a car with Paul and two women for an hour and a half didn't have much appeal to me. "I'll drive down in my own car if you don't mind," I replied. "I'll go dig up the old reports on this. I have some files and notes somewhere in my office. But seriously, don't worry too much about this. It *will* be resolved, Paul, I assure you."

I couldn't help but feel sorry for Paul, Gayle, and even Marty, too. I knew only too well that they would be apprehensive about going to court, as most civilians are, not knowing that it's often boring and tedious more than anything. They were just regular people with little experience being in a courtroom. They would be frightened by the whole endeavor, having to testify under oath, being in the hot seat, and questioned and accosted by unfriendly, stuck-up attorneys. It would be stressful for them. But I had made my living in a courtroom as a cop and later a police detective. It was a familiar environment for me. I had chewed up and spat out a lot of attorneys over the years by keeping my cool and never offering more information than was required.

They didn't scare me one bit and neither did having to testify.

Courtrooms are pretty much the same everywhere, dark paneled wood, some with marble walls, ornate ceilings, the great seal of the state, or scales of justice on the wall over the judges' raised bench. The judge can then peer down over the top of his or her glasses at the mere mortals seated in uncomfortable silence in wooden pew-like benches, like insignificant minions.

The courtroom we found ourselves in two days later, mirrored that typical image. We found that the trial actually started the following Monday with pretrial motions and the decision to have a trial by the judge without a jury. I always thought trial by judge was the best way to proceed. The judges are professional jurists and lay juries are too easily swayed, and/or deceived. They often lack common sense, good education and sometimes jurors are simply functionally illiterate people who should probably never set foot in a courtroom, for the greater good of all.

When the day came, the following week, everyone in our group was nervous. Paul was wearing a new dark blue business suit with a lighter blue dress shirt and a grey and black striped tie. Looking him over I could see he was wearing new shoes, shiny and black. He was clean and close shaved and smelled of cologne. He was trying to smile but his efforts didn't cover up the worry lines that strained his face. Gayle, the front office manager was wearing her hotel uniform, dark blue skirt, and a long-sleeved jacket and white blouse. She had only a nervous smile to offer and I could tell she was going over in her mind what she might testify about.

Marty, the PBX operator, seemed unconcerned, as her testimony would be simple and straightforward. Marty had made two phone calls on the day in question, one to the ambulance and one to the police. Perhaps Marty really did have only one dress, the same long black silk dress she always wore, bent over the PBX board, because she wore it again, for the court hearing. But her dress was clean and elegant looking, with its rustling thin black layers, and she looked the same as she always did.

I almost felt guilty being the only person who was *not* nervous. *Almost.*

In fact the courtroom seemed sort of homey and familiar. It had been a long time since I had been inside one, but I felt completely at home. Seating myself next to Paul, I looked over all the assembled people. Our hotel was represented by two attorneys, one corporate attorney, and one representing our insurance company.

Cheryl Falcone was represented by a female attorney, who wore an all black business woman's suit, with a man's necktie. Very little makeup adorned this woman's face, some eye-liner, barely visible behind solid black framed glasses, and a pale barely visible pink lipstick. She was all business, from her short haircut to her black opaque stockings. She shuffled the stack of papers in front of her, uselessly. I knew she was ready to proceed.

I could tell by the attorney's eagerness, that in her head, she had already spent her share of the millions she presumed they would naturally win. It seemed that everyone had arrived for court except Cheryl Falcone. Several women sat in the front seat of the spectators row. Mostly, they looked like they might be family members there to support Cheryl, and they were all looking around the courtroom expectantly as if waiting for someone's arrival.

I suspected Cheryl would arrive with her usual drama, but I was wrong.

The judge was also a woman. All we could see above her black robes was wire-framed, half-circle, reading glasses perched on the end of her nose. The judge wore no lipstick, and I recall she had bright pink cheeks, which made her dark eyes stand out above the reading glasses. Her long dark brown hair came to her shoulders, a sharp brown contrast to the wide streak of natural gray prominent on the right side of her head. She too shuffled a pile of papers, looking down from her throne. "Is the plaintiff ready?" she asked. Cheryl Falcone's attorney nodded and turned, motioning to a woman who was sitting in the front row behind her.

The woman glanced directly at me as she stood up and seated herself next to the attorney. This woman wore a full length dark blue dress that came clear down below her knees and just above her ankles. Her blouse was pale gray, shiny like it was made of satin with a starched white Peter Pan collar. What could be seen of her legs were covered by brown cotton stockings which were crumpled at the ankle, making the stockings appear slightly too large. Her hair, suspiciously more gray than light brown, was done up in a bun and covered by a white crocheted snood.

The woman appeared for all the world like a schoolmarm or a plain Jane librarian. Who *was* this woman we all wondered? Then it became clear and I was shocked. I think we were *all* shocked.

The woman was Cheryl Falcone!

But this was *not* the Cheryl Falcone any of us remembered. This was not the heavily perfumed, sexy-girl, with the crotch-tight slacks and see-through flesh-colored blouse that I rescued from the man with the gun. Paul looked very confused, looking over at me curiously, his eyes, anxious. "What's going on?" he whispered. "Who *is* that?!"

I was used to people dressing up to go to court, but *this* Cheryl Falcone was over the top. In an obvious costume, made over to convince the court that the big bad hotel had done nothing to prevent this poor matronly woman from being robbed by the nasty man with the gun, Cheryl had completely changed her look. I was not surprised.

"I'm pretty sure that's Cheryl!" I whispered back to Paul, laughing under my breath. He stared at her in disbelief even more apprehensive then looked at me slightly offended. "How can you laugh at a time like this?" he hissed under his breath. "Paul, you need to relax and watch the show!" I said with an indulgent smile. "What do you mean?!" Paul shot back. "Paul, this is *my* turf. Trust me. Do you know how many courtrooms I've been in? It's all theater, don't worry so much."

"What do you mean don't worry?!"

I could tell Paul was fearful that the woman judge, the woman attorney and now this other matronly woman he hadn't initially recognized had all conspired together, and that the hotel was naturally doomed to a huge scandal and the resulting bankruptcy. His eyes darted back and forth, glancing at all three women intermittently, and he seemed extremely concerned, almost distraught. Paul was hoping for some comforting glances from our attorneys but found none, when they glanced in our direction, stony faced and annoyed.

"Paul, you gotta relax. Trust me. It's not gonna be as bad as you think."

"Are you sure?"

The costumed female sitting with the lady attorney glanced back at me. Her chin was slightly raised in quiet defiance. It was Cheryl alright. Her eyes were the same — with that knowing, conspiratorial expression of hers. I could even see the vestiges of old mascara still clumped together on her eyelashes, from where she had not properly taken off all her make-up, probably that morning, in her hurry to get to court. She had tried to come off looking like a nun, but couldn't quite pull it off, and came off looking like what she was — a sometime party girl who had tried to dumb down her appearance for a court hearing.

Gayle leaned forward and looked over at me questioningly, wondering if it was indeed the same sexy, Cheryl Falcone she had checked in at the counter during her unfortunate stay at the Benson. "Is that her?" she mouthed in my direction. I mouthed back "Yes!" while nodding my head meaningfully, and grinning slightly. Gayle then leaned back and sighed heavily with a disgusted look on her face.

Marty the PBX operator was the only one who seemed to be having any fun. She had never seen Cheryl in person so didn't quite understand our consternation. She continued to stare about the room, unconcerned and pleased, enjoying the spectacle and entertainment of an out of the ordinary, out of town experience.

Gathering my bearings, I could see the opposition's obvious plan, I knew exactly how to defend our case. This might even be fun. After some preliminary formalities and chatter between the judge and the clerk, Cheryl was called to the stand to testify first. She was sworn to tell the truth, the whole truth and nothing but the truth. She then seated herself carefully in the hardback wooden chair, pulling and smoothing down her skirt, adjusting herself in the chair, fixing her collar and folding her hands on her lap. She looked as prim and proper as a stereotype of a virginal school teacher saving souls in the Deep South.

Cheryl was visible only from the waist up and with a swish at her hair, she adjusted the snood, cleared her throat and the fairytale began. She told the judge that she had been a traveling sales representative for a cosmetics company, Fabergé, and always stayed at the Benson Hotel when traveling to Portland. As I recall she claimed she had dined alone at *Jake's famous*

Crawfish that night, which was a nice seafood restaurant a few blocks away. She claimed when she was finished, she began her leisurely walk back to her hotel room at the Benson.

To the best of my recollection, Cheryl told the judge that when she was about two blocks from the hotel she noticed a white man had begun following her. Nervous, she quickened her step and by the time she entered the front door, the gray haired man was directly behind her. She said she felt "safer" once she was in the hotel lobby. But the man hovered behind her, she said, as she prepared to walk into the elevator. At the last minute, she said, he pushed by her and into the elevator. She had already pressed the ninth floor call button by then, but claimed she was trapped. She was trapped and the man scared her. He then began to push and pull at her, demanding her money and crowding her into the corner of the elevator. He wouldn't let her move, she said, or escape.

Cheryl continued with her testimony, claiming that she was hoping the elevator would stop and someone would get on and help her, but no one did. When the elevator stopped on the ninth floor, she claimed she pushed past the man and ran down the corridor toward her room. But he caught her arm in front of her room and began hitting her with a "big gun" and demanding her money. She then concluded that at that point, she was bleeding and thought she was going to be killed. She was so scared, she said in conclusion.

Cheryl was sobbing by then, quite convincingly, and wiping her eyes with a crumpled Kleenex. I wondered if she had taken drama in high school or college, her performance was that good. "And what happened then?" her attorney asked, her voice patient and full of syrupy compassion. Cheryl claimed that the hotel security officer showed up and the man with the gun ran off.

Adding that no one even tried to catch the man, she further claimed, her voice squealing in fake distress. She looked around her and fluttered her eyelashes. The attorney gazed sympathetically at Cheryl as she mopped at her tears with the soaked Kleenex. "What happened next?" asked the attorney.

As the questions continued, Cheryl said she was taken to a hospital and the cut on her forehead was stitched up. She then stated that she was left with a disfiguring scar. She pulled back her hair and pointed at the side of her head. "It's permanent!" Cheryl wailed. Paul was now leaning forward, his elbows on his knees and his head in his hands and a dismal look of defeat on his face. I was nonplussed, however. I had witnessed scenes like this many times before and while Paul thought it was all real, *and* the end of the world, I knew it to be the performance that it was.

Radio commentator Paul Harvey, (1918-2009) was famous for stopping his yarn mid-story to play the commercial, usually a soap or flour commercial, and when he returned on the air, he would famously say: "And now for the *rest* of the story!" I was the rest of the story in *this* colorful drama, and I could hardly wait to get on the stand and tell *my* side of things and what I had witnessed and experienced.

I watched amused, as Cheryl was excused from the stand. She got up, and stood for a moment, and then swayed slightly, as if she might faint. I thought she should get an Oscar for her performance. It was absurd, shameless and transparent.

When I was called to the stand, I walked over and sat down, ready to get down to business. "How are you employed Mr. DuPay?" asked the short-haired, necktied female attorney. "I'm Director of Security for the Benson Hotel," I answered politely, with a smile. "And what is your background, Mr. DuPay, what makes you *qualified* for this job?" she asked with a knowing glance at the judge and a condescending smirk for me. Wow, I thought to myself, this lady hasn't done her homework — so I let her have it right between the eyes.

As I recall, I said, "I was a Portland police officer, Ma'am. A street cop for six years before being promoted to detective in 1967 when I was 31. From there I worked the next eleven years of my time with PPB in burglary and finally in the homicide detail," putting emphasis on the word *homicide*.

Obviously surprised, the attorney's eyes dropped to the table in front of her as if she were searching for something, or contemplating her next move. She must have thought I was just some bumbling gumshoe Rent-a-cop, security guard, with only a high school diploma and no college. She couldn't have been more wrong.

I felt like telling her that good attorneys never ask a question they don't already know the answer to, but decided against it. I remember her saying, "Let's just get to the incident where Ms. Falcone was attacked by the robber with the gun. Tell the court what happened.". The spectators were now sitting on the edge of their seats listening with greater interest. They must have initially thought I was a Rent-a-cop, but not anymore. I testified that I was patrolling the ninth floor guestroom corridor when I heard a woman scream. I ran in the direction of the commotion and heard what sounded like a blow to the head with a metal object.

"How did you know it was a metal object? asked the attorney. I told her that it clanked. It sounded like metal hitting someone on the head. I had heard people being pistol whipped before, when I was a police officer, I explained, and I knew what it sounds like.

Then she asked me: "You must have seen the robbery as it was happening, is that right?" The attorney was trying to suggest that what happened was a robbery, a typical lawyer maneuver. "It was not a robbery," I declared flatly, staring straight into the attorney's eyes who now looked more confused than ever.

"Well, uh..." the lawyer stammered. She claimed that her client had *assured* her she was beaten during a robbery. I could tell the attorney was losing her stride. *"It wasn't a robbery,"* I repeated calmly. My words seemed to drop on the hardwood table like the proverbial ton of bricks. Everyone looked confused, turning their heads and looking at each other for answers. Exasperated now, the lady attorney asked how I could be sure it *wasn't* a robbery.

The question was perfect and I had been waiting for it. I had led Cheryl's attorney right down the garden path and I was about to spring the trap. I explained what the man with the gun had said explicitly. "The man said 'Gimme *my* money!' He didn't say 'Gimme *your* money!' He said 'gimme *MY* money." A silence descended on the court room like a heavy blanket. The case was over and everyone in the room knew it, Yet her lawyer stammered on. The lawyer made a rookie mistake. She asked a question she didn't already know the answer to — a foolish error.

"I don't see how that proves…" she began.

I explained that my experience as a detective, having worked in several drug stings, had informed my opinion. I told her that what likely happened was some kind of a transaction between the two of them that had not gone well. The guy didn't want *her* money, he wanted *his* money. I told her I could only speculate on what he may have sold her, but I'd wager it was drugs, specifically, and likely cocaine. I sat comfortably and then glanced across at the judge, unconcerned. The attorney looked down at the counsel table, unsure of what question to ask next, as our attorneys began shuffling papers, trying to hide duel smirks. They liked the way things were proceeding.

"What did you see next Mr. DuPay?" the attorney asked in a defeated tone.

Once again Cheryl's attorney stuck her head in the noose. I had to wonder how much experience she had in courtrooms to be so naïve. It was *the* question I had been waiting for. I responded, explaining that I had seen a heavyset man with short gray hair, holding a .45 automatic pistol in a raised position. He was about to strike a woman crouched on the floor, with her arms upraised defensively. I explained that she was wearing tight black slacks, and was heavily made up with cosmetics. The blouse she was wearing was transparent and was torn from the altercation and she was without a bra as I could clearly see both of her breasts through the sheer fabric.

I further explained that I saw blood coming from her lower lip, and another cut on her forehead, which was also bleeding. I continued, saying that the mascara she was wearing was smeared from perspiration and from her tears.

The attorney sighed.

"Did you chase the robber away?" asked the attorney, with growing impatience. I explained again that I did not believe it was not a robbery. "The man was demanding *his* money not *hers,* but when he saw me, he ran down the corridor and ran out onto the fire exit."

"Did you chase the man with the gun?" she asked. "No. Catching the armed man would be the job of the police. I'm no longer a sworn police officer. My obligation was to obtain immediate medical assistance for Ms. Falcone and protect her in her injured state, which I did."

By the time I was finished testifying, I could tell by the expression on the judge's face that she realized Cheryl Falcone had been lying all along. I had very carefully skirted around the attorney's language that suggested Cheryl was *robbed* rather than what had really happened. What had actually happened, in my opinion, was that Cheryl was buying dope from the man and had tried to shortchange him for it. After the altercation and violent assault happened, it was clear Cheryl thought she'd just make some quick cash by suing the Benson Hotel for the comical sum of one million dollars.

Why not think big, right? If she could blame the hotel for what happened, and pin the problem on the Benson because they had not provided "reasonable care" then she might come into some quick cash. In the end, and after some thinking, I felt the judge was able to read between the lines, too. Judges become very familiar with the subtext of testimony. They know what goes *unsaid* can lead to an entirely different truth and judges are often quite good at reading people who are lying.

Our attorneys alluded to the fact that some kind of a "transaction," had indeed gone wrong and that the scantily dressed Cheryl Falcone was the *real* Cheryl Falcone and not the woman sitting presently before the court. *That* woman was a costumed actress with her hair done up in a severe bun, and tightly wrapped up in a matronly snood. She was sans lipstick or makeup of any kind in a floor length skirt and clearly posing as a timid Plain Jane. A point by point presentation was made by our attorneys carefully outlining the requirement of *reasonable care* and that I had indeed provided reasonable care, and the case was rested.

The judge was looking at the clock, our attorneys were looking at the clock. It was over. Cheryl's attorney was watching *her* share of the settlement money go down the drain with the dish soap, and Cheryl was looking at me with an evil glare. She knew it was all because of me. I had ruined her *sure thing* case all by myself. I gazed back at her impassively, expressionless and calm.

Paul looked confused. He wasn't sure if things had gone well or not. He was worried that three women, the judge, Cheryl and her attorney might equate to a stacked deck against him. I thought we would win, but then going to court was always a crapshoot and we would have to wait until tomorrow for a verdict. But I wasn't worried — I figured the judge would see right through Cheryl.

As we all filed out of the courtroom, all I wanted was to go back to the hotel and have a stiff whiskey and a good dinner. Boss-man and hotel owner, Lynn Himmelman, would be paying for it and I would be enjoying it fully. At Paul's suggestion, Marty, Gayle and I had dinner in my room so we could talk about the lawsuit privately. I had whiskey before dinner and everyone ordered prime rib, baked potatoes, and excellent green salads. For dessert, I had a pear and cottage cheese salad *and* Crème Brulee, stuffing myself again.

Paul ordered two bottles of wine, one red and one white and they arrived properly iced in silver ice buckets wrapped with a white towel. As we ate, and drank wine, the conversation focused on how I thought the trial had gone and if I thought we'd won. By now they all thought I was an expert on trials, and they looked at me expectantly, trying to get some of the relaxed feeling I had, as if it might rub off on them. I couldn't help but feel amused. They were green and filled with anxiety, and I was the Old Hand expert. I felt the trial had gone well for us, and that I had done the best I could to make Cheryl look unreliable. I told them it would work out in our favor and not to worry.

"Are you sure, Don?" I was asked more than once. "I don't expect any problems," I said calmly. I had always been certain that the assault was over a dope-deal-gone-bad, and that Cheryl Falcone was trying to save face with her cosmetics company. I reminded them that Cheryl, on more than one occasion, wiggled provocatively through the hotel lobby, followed by a wafting cloud of her strong perfume, not because I was trying to demonize her for being provocative, but merely point out that she looked more like a high-class call girl than a professional working woman with a reputation to protect. Clearly, she liked attention.

I reminded them that she often drank too much, was provocative to the point of being ridiculous and was in my opinion, definitely a party girl. Yet it was impossible to be sure what would happen, and we would just have to wait for the judge to sleep on it. Paul filled our wine glasses and we toasted to a victory. Then we toasted again as everyone began to finally relax.

When the bottles of wine were drained and empty, Paul loosened his tie and his worried look changed to cautious optimism. "Maybe we'll be okay?" he said, more as a question than a statement, wiping his mouth with a napkin. "Yes, maybe we *will* be okay!" he repeated to himself. He nodded, stood up, and with a half bow, excused himself, leaving to go to his room.

Marty excused herself next, saying she wasn't used to all this excitement and she would be off to bed, but she paused first, stopping to make a call to the Benson on the house phone. She smiled at me and without speaking into the phone, hung the receiver up. "Just making sure my PBX operators are answering the phone properly," she explained, and with a 'good evening' wave she disappeared out the door.

Marty was indeed the voice of the Benson Hotel.

Gayle and I were now left alone sitting next to each other on the couch. She opened the bottle of white wine and poured us each a glass. She seemed inclined to chat and I was feeling relaxed and idle and more than willing to listen. As Security Director I rarely socialized with other hotel staff as it could make my job impossible if I became too friendly with the enemy. But we were out of town, comfortable on the couch, bellies full of prime rib and potatoes, and with one bottle of wine downed, and one to go, maybe we could relax and just talk.

Gayle had been a farm girl growing up in rural Colorado, to strict religious parents and she was expected to be a good Christian woman. That meant marrying and having a lot of little "farm hands" as she recalled her mother saying. She confided that she escaped Colorado, and a farm life of pigs, rabbits, and wiping the poop off the fresh chicken eggs, and ran away to "the big city." I laughed when she explained that *Portland* was "the big city" she had escaped to, as most native Portlanders recognize it for the small town that it is.

Gayle found work as a night auditor on the graveyard shift at the old but elegant Multnomah Hotel, which was located on 3rd and Pine, and is now the site of the Embassy Hotel. She eventually found a better job at the Benson and ultimately was promoted to front office manager. Gayle had never married, had no children and confessed she fully expected to live to be an old maid and that was fine with her. It is interesting, I thought, how wine not only warms the tongue but wipes away inhibitions much as the quick swipe of a bar towel wipes away the remnants of the previous customer's presence.

I told her of my similar upbringing on a farm in Montana and that my family moved us to the "big city," when I was just eleven and we moved to Portland. With relaxed inhibitions, we sat closer together, leaning on each other, drinking the wine, and swapping stories. I told her of my time as a farm kid, shooting gophers and rabbits, cutting off the heads of chickens for my mother, for our Sunday dinner and enduring the Montana cold and snow, lack of electricity, the smelly outhouse and the danger of the kerosene lamps.

I told her how we had used genuine inkwells in the old one-room schoolhouse where I learned to read and write cursive with nibbed writing pens. During the time I was learning cursive writing, my sisters and I had also learned how to ice skate on a frozen creek and had many fun times in the Montana cold.

I remember waking up several hours later, a little hazy. Her head was on my shoulder, her mouth was slightly open, and we were holding hands. The bed was unrumpled and there was still an inch of wine remaining in the bottle. Not wanting to wake her, and risk the chance of someone seeing her leave my room in the middle of the night, I eased myself off the couch and covered her with a blanket. She smelled really good, from a nice understated floral perfume, and I watched her sleep for a moment.

If there was a stiff and stifled old maid in Gayle yearning for release, it would have to come out at a different time. She was a nice girl I decided, looking for the right man, but it wouldn't be me. I just didn't think of her in that way and regarded her as something akin to a beloved sister. I sat on the edge of my bed, slugged down the remaining wine, eased over to the center of the bed and fell into a comfortable sleep, fully dressed.

The Trial Continued with Everyone a Jumble of Nerves

The following day we all lumbered into the courtroom. Everyone was nervous, edgy, anxious. Everyone except me.

Of course we ended up winning the lawsuit, amidst quiet cheers and many broad smiles as Cheryl Falcone's lawsuit was dismissed. I was nonplussed at the victory. I *knew* we would win. There was never a moment when I seriously worried about losing, mostly because Cheryl had made such a poor impression. She was a terrible actress and if *overacting* could have been an artform, she had it downpat. Mostly, it was her self-important *entitlement* that shone through, which lost her the case.

Cheryl Falcone received no money. Plus she was ordered to pay our attorneys a bill of around $10,000 dollars. She would have to arrange a payment plan and would be paying that debt off for a few years, I suspected.

We returned to the Benson as conquering heros. Everyone at the Benson knew the news, even before we arrived back. They all wanted to shake our hands and loaded us up with pats on the back and many smiles and "congratulations!" I even received a "Goot on you!" from a smiling and happy Chef Bauser, his warbled and charming attempt at "Good for you!" It was the first nice thing Bauser had ever uttered to me in the entire time I'd known him and I couldn't help but smile.

The whole experience left me with a renewed sense of involvement and commitment to the Benson hotel. "The corporate office is really pleased!" offered Paul, tentatively patting me on the shoulder, the following day, a look of sheepish admiration on his face. I took that remark to mean that his father was happy about the outcome, because I'm sure his father knew every detail. The truth is we had won the case *because* of me.

If I had not testified in the way I did, saying the things I said, exactly as I said them, we might have lost. It helped that Cheryl Falcone made such a bad impression, but I knew my leadership was the real reason the Benson Hotel had not paid through the nose.

I'm sure there was an added swagger in my walk, as I made my way around the corridors for the next few days. But the reality was, although I had done everything correctly when I heard the first scream by Cheryl, I also knew it was *pure luck* that I had been on the ninth floor at the time of the assault. Had I not been perfectly located to respond, had I been in the basement for instance, Cheryl Falcone may have been killed, or at least further injured and surely would have won a large settlement against the hotel.

In that sense the Benson had dodged a bullet; a bullet the size of a cannon ball. If I had not been there, we might have had a dead woman to deal with, and the hotel would have had to pay a fortune in damages, and pay *again* with the loss of our good reputation.

Dealing With the Law of Averages

Even the crying beggar lady Laurie, the Charles Laughton look alike, knew I couldn't be everywhere all the time. I needed a heftier staff, and I needed regular working hours. Popping in at all hours of the day and night, and calling unexpected fire drills was getting to be too much of a burden. I was a good man but I was only *one* man. I needed some support.

So, I did my homework. What would it cost to add one or two more security officers? How much coverage in terms of shifts and days would I get hiring two more people? How could having more staff better manage the risks inherent in running this big hotel? I decided adding only one more security officer would do little good, I would need at least two. I would try for two at first, then later hope to add a third in the future.

With my ducks all in a row and costs figured out, I knocked on Paul's office door several days later. I fully expected to be put off with the answer I had come to expect from bureaucrats and top managers, which would be something like: "Sorry, we just can't afford it at this time. Perhaps later."

"Come in Don!" said Paul through the door, "I've been expecting you." Crap! I thought. He's just waiting to shoot me down. His father had already told him not to spend any more money. Well, it was after all *their* money and *their* reputation, and *their* hotel. I would continue to do the best job I could, as I always had. "Que Será, Será!"as the expression goes.

I was surprised when Paul greeted me with a smile on his face, and stood up offering his hand. "It's good to see you, Don!" he said. "I've been talking with our attorneys and the corporate office in Seattle. They think it would be wise for the Benson to add more security and probably some surveillance cameras too, so we could have a video record of the lobby activities."

Wow! It is amazing how getting slapped with a huge lawsuit can make a company sit up and pay attention. I took a deep breath, smiled, and told him I anticipated the need and already had calculated some figures to look at. Except for the surveillance cameras of course, but I kept that part to myself.

While I was sitting there, Paul called personnel and told them to put an ad in the paper for two security officer positions, to be hired and trained by the Director of Security. "I know you will get us two good people, Don! And congratulations again for the way you handled yourself at the trial. It made all the difference in the world to the Benson!"

I backed out of his office door smiling, slapping my papers together, almost victoriously against my palm. That had been too easy. Now, I would be a real department head, with staff and cameras. Ah yes, cameras! I had always wanted one in the basement watching the kitchen activities and the room service cashiers as well as the lobby. As a detective, my colleagues and I had used hidden cameras to do several "stings" on a Portland pawn shop, so I was familiar with cameras and how they operated. Half empty bottles of wine were still being taken out the employee entrance on the Oak street side of the building — not to mention other things that would wind up missing regularly from the kitchen, can openers, bottle openers, full salt and pepper shakers.

Some of the waitstaff figured the wine had already been paid for, so why not take the leftovers home? And the accounting department informed me there had been recent problems with small amounts of money missing from the room service cash register. With cameras I could stop some of the losses and promote better behavior among the employees.

The newspaper ad placed in the *Oregonian Newspaper* produced several applicants and the personnel office scheduled appointments for interviews. There were three or four applicants who thought hotel security might be a policeman's job, along with a hippy with scraggly long hair wearing round John Lennon eyeglasses. He wanted night work while attending college, and thought he would be a good candidate for the job. I wanted someone with no security experience because I would teach them all they needed to know, my way, and as this position was *not* a police job, I didn't want someone with preconceived ideas on how it *should* be done. I didn't want any Cop Wannabes and quickly ruled them out. I wanted a clean slate.

The successful applicant I wanted had to have the right look, be clean-cut, articulate and cool under fire. They had to look like they *belonged* in a high class hotel like the Benson. They had to have some class of their own because they would be interacting with mostly affluent, successful people. Some of those people might be indulging in a little innocent misbehavior, for the simple reason that they were out-of-town and looking for a good time.

The applicant I wanted had to be a *diplomat* who understood how to be discreet.

On my second day of interviews I found the right guy! His name was Victor and he was Hispanic. Born in Los Angeles, he looked like he belonged in a three piece suit. He wore a pencil-thin mustache, had a quick easy smile, and was extremely handsome with perfect teeth and even features. His black hair was neatly trimmed, and shiny from Brylcreem. Victor was muscular, always gave me direct eye contact, was an ex-Marine and had that confidence, and upright bearing that comes with someone who's served in the military. I hired him on the spot, pending a background check, knowing as I did that he would be *perfect* for the job.

The personnel department told me there were two applications from women and would I consider hiring a woman? Of course I would. But only the *right* woman. "Set up the appointments, please!" I said. The first applicant was the best and I hired her, too. Her name was Norma. Norma was classy, in her fifties, looked matronly, and trustworthy. She was the mom-next-door type. Her hair was silver gray and short, just covering her ears. Her blue eyes were clearly visible over slightly gray tinted glasses, which slipped down her nose a bit as we talked. As the glasses slipped down, she was looking at me over the top of them which gave her that *'don't-you-dare-talk-back-to-me'* school teacher look. She was perfect.

I could just visualize her looking over the top of those tinted glasses, telling one of our wealthy patrons it was time to go to their room. "No more drinking this evening, honey!" she would say. Norma was the type of matron that could call any-one "honey," and get away with it. She was a widow looking for extra income, and wanted to work in "a nice place like the Benson," she told me. I was impressed. After the two applicants' background checks turned out okay, I put Victor and Norma both on the payroll, and spent the next two weeks breaking them into the hotel environment and introducing them to the staff.

Victor would wear a black or blue three piece suit and Norma would wear a dark blue lady's business suit with a white blouse and Peter Pan collar. They wore black name tags with gold letters. Chef Bauser was as polite as Bauser could be to the new employee's, a brief glance and a nod in their general direction was about all he could muster. "Velcom to da Benson," he muttered, reluctantly, when I introduced him to Victor and Norma.

Charlotte, our exotic cocktail waitress, smiled politely and gave them each a soft accented, "Hello, and welcome to the Benson!" She stared a little longer at Victor, who looked sharp in his suit. "Are you like him?" she asked, nodding in my direction, "I mean, when it comes to being prudish about serving alcohol?" Charlotte winked at me and I waited for Victor to answer the question. A bright smile suddenly spread over his face. "I'm exactly like Don, just younger," he answered, smartly.

Then the smile dropped off his face, as quickly as it had appeared and was replaced with a business-like stare. Charlotte looked Norma over politely also and received Norma's look in return, the 'over the top of her glasses look' but with a smile. I was sure that either of my new security officers could handle any problems in the lobby lounge if a drunken fight broke out and someone had to be escorted out.

As I trained them, I answered their questions and concerns, explaining firmly that we were *not* police officers, but only "risk managers," politely enforcing hotel policy. I made sure part of their training entailed reading all they could on hotel lawsuits until they had a thorough understanding of exactly what "reasonable care" meant.

I made it clear that they were *not* to behave like police officers. That was not their or my job, but only the job of a trained and "sworn police officer," I explained. You could get into a lot of trouble pretending to be a cop and you couldn't get carried away with thinking you possessed the authority of a police officer. Only a *sworn* police officer could do certain things, or arrest someone, "and that's not us!" I told them.

We reviewed the recent Cheryl Falcone lawsuit over lunch one day, and I made sure they knew exactly why we had prevailed in court. I explained that running a large luxury hotel, like any business, had certain risks and our job was to *manage* those risks like keeping undesirables off the premises as they may be more than just annoying, but mentally ill and dangerous to the clientèle.

I explained the enormous monetary value of the liquor license to the hotel and why we must be vigilant in not allowing *any* patron to be overserved or anyone to remove alcohol from the premises, which included guests *and* employees.

After ten days of spending every hour with them, I felt safe in turning them loose. I also asked Gayle, the Front Office Manager, to keep an eye on them, and make sure they didn't get into trouble. And I asked Marty in PBX to make sure they responded to radio calls in a timely manner. Then I went home and slept for twenty four hours straight. I was exhausted.

Later, the next day, I further joked with Janet, the purchase agent, that I hoped Chef Bauser wouldn't try to eat one of them, angrily carving them up with one of his serrated edged knives, while in the midst of one of his notorious fits of rage. She laughed and said he probably would not.

The surveillance cameras were the next security measure to make the Benson a safer place as it added eyes on the lobby and the basement kitchen-employee exit area. The camera views were fed into a 24-hour continuous video recorder. The lobby camera provided a full view of the lobby, and monitored all persons arriving or leaving the hotel. As I helped install most of the camera's, I positioned the basement camera so it had a full view of the room service cash register. This camera had an extra wide-angle lens so although it was monitoring room service, it could also see into Chef Bauser's kitchen as well as any arriving and departing employees.

Above the camera, on the wall, I affixed a large bright yellow smiley face sticker that read: "Smile, you're on camera!" I hoped it would discourage employee theft. I stood back, looking at the new camera with some satisfaction only to hear the clip-clop of Chef Bauser's wooden clogs coming up behind me.

Pretending to ignore him I didn't move and continued looking up at the camera. He clogged around me so that he was standing directly in front of me. "Vhy you vat-chink me?!" he demanded, getting a little red in the face, and pointing up at the shiny new camera staring down at us. I stepped back, feigning all the innocence my face could muster and replied, "Oh, it's not for you. Mr. Mannerly wanted a surveillance camera to watch room service, to prevent theft. It's certainly not to watch you, Chef Bauser!"

Then I leaned forward and whispered: "Confidentially, some money *has* been missing from the cash register, so we have to be careful." Pushing my luck a little more, I gave him a knowing nudge in the ribs, with my elbow as I turned to go. Bauser's face warped into an instant frown of anger and general disgust at the sight of me, and again we were back to him hating my guts.

I knew he didn't believe me when I said the camera was not for him, but since I blamed the camera on Paul, Bauser was stuck with my answer. Part of me felt satisfied. I had just pushed Chef Superstar a little off center and he was not comfortable there. Bauser turned around and stomped back to the kitchen, muttering something in his foreign tongue, which I didn't understand. I figured it probably wasn't very nice.

More of the Rich & Famous
Seeing & Being Seen

The Benson Hotel was the home of the rich and famous. Some, like golfing great Arnold Palmer were regulars and we got to know him on a first name basis. I didn't realize that Portland had so many golf tournaments, but it seemed like Mr. Palmer was at the Benson about every month or so. He seemed to be a regular guy, and always took time to have a pleasant conversation with the doorman while waiting for his limousine to pull up in front. Many of the rich and famous were self-important and stuffy, but not Arnold. He always had a smile for the staff, and for me, and tipped well I was told.

Waylon Jennings, on the other hand, *was* rich and stuffy and had a heavy no-nonsense security detail of several mean looking white men. His security guys dressed in black Frisco jeans, black t-shirts, black leather gloves, and had radios with earbuds. They were big 'good ole' boys, tall and muscular, all with Ozark style beards, which gave them a fearsome appearance. Waylon himself was whisked through the lobby surrounded on all sides by these numerous bodies, all dressed in black and into his waiting limousine.

Barely a glimpse of Jennings could be seen, and he never smiled, never spoke to the staff, and took all his meals in his suite. He only stayed at the hotel once during my tenure but I got the feeling his entourage wasn't comfortable this far up North in Or-ee-gone. I wondered what he had done to deserve such a security detail. He had to have made some enemies in his time, as he'd been a methamphetamine and cocaine addict since the 1960s. He finally sobered up, so the rumor goes right around 1984, which would have been sometime after he came to the Benson Hotel on his trip to Portland.

Millionaire oil man and philanthropist Armand Hammer also visited the Benson and spoke at a fundraising dinner there for a charity he supported. I stood in the doorway of the Mayfair Room where his event was held just to see the man and listen to him speak. He introduced himself as Armand Hammer, "the baking soda man!" The audience laughed as he went on to explain that he was so often asked if he was the baking soda guy, that he actually bought stock in the Arm & Hammer company just so he could say, "Yes. I'm that guy." The audience laughed and so did I, as I found it a charming way to break the ice before a serious speech asking folks for money for his charity.

The staff was delighted when the beloved Ella Fitzgerald visited the hotel while on a concert tour that included Portland. She appeared in the lobby, looking older than she did on television, and tired. Her hair was curled and piled on her head, and her makeup was professionally applied and looked perfect. Ella wore thick eye glasses, in large frames, which brought atten-tion to her lustrous brown eyes, long lashes, and the shimmer-ing blue eyeshadow she favored.

Ella was dressed in an elegant black dressing-gown as she walked around the lobby, stopping to chat with folks who recognized her. Her legs were adorned by black opaque hose and her feet looked comfortable in her well-worn fuzzy ivory-white slippers. Yes, the diva was wearing slippers that looked like they were the old ones she wore at home.

Ella was attended by her companion and assistant, a short, younger Black woman who held her arm as she walked, helping to steady her. The assistant had a wary, but friendly look that left no doubt that she was looking out for Ella, and you'd better be respectful or else. Ella signed a few autographs for those bold enough to approach her, and then disappeared across the lobby and into the elevators.

I couldn't help noticing how fame and fortune affected celebrities differently. When comparing Ella and her one person security detail to that of the pompous Waylon Jennings, with his huge entourage acting like they were the secret service, or movie stars being hounded by the paparazzi looking to cash in on photos, I saw how pompous some celebrities are, while others are genuinely humble, appreciative people.

Ella came from poverty and a broken home and was orphaned at the age of fifteen, when her mother Temperance, "Tempie" died of a heart attack in 1932 after a serious car accident. Ella took the loss of her mother hard and was placed in the *Colored Orphan Asylum* which was located in the Bronx. She didn't stay long, and ended up in the *New York Training School for Girls*. Later the school, much like the orphanage, was exposed as a terrible place where random abuse of minor girls was common. She soon left the training school, and lived on the streets of

NY, all during the Great Depression until she found a better situation. After she became wealthy, Ella donated huge sums of money to local charities in NY that helped support orphaned girls, particularly. Ella Fitzgerald was definitely the kind of celebrity who had not forgotten her origins, nor how to be a gracious, dignified and compassionate person. Her lasting legacy was that she would help many thousands of NY girls who may have grown up just as she had.

Some Great Benson Employees I will Never Forget

I often said Marty was the voice of the Benson, but if Marty was the voice of the Benson, then Jim Gimarelli was the face and handshake of the Benson Hotel. As the long time Benson Concierge, Jim was a magician. If a guest was upset about something, or needed something, Jim got it fixed. If a guest needed something special, Jim made it happen. I thought of Jim Gimarelli as a human Google search engine of his time.

Ask "Jim-Jim" and the answer popped up from his smiling face. He knew what was going on in Portland and eagerly shared information whenever he was asked. He was a consummate gentleman with a genuine smile, flashed easily in conversation. His voice was a resonant baritone, but he spoke softly, almost confidentially, which made people feel special when they were around him. When I talked with Jim it seemed like we were two buddies, sharing secrets. Jim's gift was that he made everyone feel *they* were sharing a secret too. One barely noticed his thinning dark hair, just his smile, outstretched hand, and friendly helpful demeanor.

Jim worked from a walnut desk with a red telephone, in the lobby near the foot of the grand staircase. As I came to know Jim I inquired if male guests ever asked him to provide a female companion for an overnight stay. I was curious because it was a fairly regular occurrence that some guy would ask one of the waiters.

Jim reflected for a moment and answered honestly. "Yes, Don," he replied, "I have been asked that, but I always shrug my shoulders and politely say, "No-Can-Do." Then almost as an afterthought he added, "You know Don, if I ever helped in that way, why that would make me a pimp. And you know, I would never do *anything* to destroy the impeccable reputation of the Benson Hotel." And I believed him, as we stood together and both chuckled. Not once did I hear even a whisper that Jim Gimarelli had arranged anything improper in all his years with the Benson.

Jim did me a favor once that I never forgot, which illustrated perfectly how caring and generous he was. A family reunion was being held in Seattle and I wanted to arrive in grand style, in a car better looking than my small import. Jim arranged with his preferred car rental agency for me to drive a rented Cadillac at Chevrolet prices. It made my trip affordable and fun. Jim Gimarelli became, if not an icon, then certainly a fixture of the Benson Hotel. Jim worked there for over twenty incredible years, and I sometimes joked that he was hired by Simon Benson himself, he had such old world charm. Jim was a classy guy and is well remembered in the minds of the many people who knew and worked with him as being a consummate gentleman who everybody loved.

Every Wednesday at two in the afternoon, the "Department Head Meeting" was held on the ninth floor in the Comptroller's office. This office had a meeting table big enough to accommodate all nine of us, plus Paul. I didn't mind the meetings as it was just an hour of listening to the other department heads air their various issues, concerns or problems.

One memorable Wednesday we had our usual meeting. On this day, our Purchasing Agent Janet, reminded us to fill out purchase orders for our needed supplies. We all smiled and kind of chuckled at that, because Paul, the hotel manager, often had a habit of *not* signing the purchase orders in a timely manner.

Perhaps somewhere in his mind, he thought he might be saving money by not signing them, and putting off the inevitable. But he was merely causing a lot of frustration for our Purchasing Agent, Janet. Once, only a few weeks before this weekly meeting, my purchase order for staples and paper clips had been ignored for over three weeks. I retaliated by buying my own and then joking about it to some of the other employee's. It finally got back to Paul and I remember he was none too pleased.

At the Wednesday meeting, the Executive Housekeeper told us she had to purchase a whopping 1000 new sets of our regular pink bed linen and that the price had gone up yet again. I offered the obvious suggestion that white linen would be cheaper, if the hotel *really* wanted to save money. My suggestion was met with little enthusiasm by the other department heads. Tradition, I was informed, required the trademark Benson Hotel *pink* to be included in the choice of all bed linen.

Our sales manager, whose name was also Don, was constantly seeking new business for the hotel by booking conventions requiring many rooms and lavish banquets, but Chef Bauser complained that the number of large banquets, regularly scheduled, was taxing his staff and he might need to hire more cooks, which could be costly. Don Chambers was very professional and a clear asset to the Benson. He indicated that he had been investigating the possibility of encouraging more traveling Japanese businessmen to book rooms for more revenue at the hotel and would be booking a week-long visit to Tokyo, to do some marketing in the next few days, for just that purpose. We all agreed that would be a great idea, and might bring in even more important clients.

Next, Paul has some news to share. He seemed excited about it, but it would take a while for him to get to it. Paul was a scuba diver and would occasionally show off several of the ugly fish he had speared while scuba diving in Hood Canal in Washington state, a deep water canal used by Navy submarines. He had actually dragged some of these cold, smelly fish into the Benson for the sole purpose of showing them off to his fellow co-workers.

I'd have been too afraid to get in that nasty water, spear or no spear. I'd have been too chicken. But not Paul. He was never afraid to go scuba diving in dangerous, freezing waters!

At the end of that meeting, with all the mundane business resolved for the time being, Paul stood up and leaned against his chair to address us. He seemed a little more animated, with an 'I've got a secret' smile on his face, and he alternated between an attempt at seriousness and his attempts to control an underlying excitement.

Paul was trying to maintain his usual formality, but it was obvious he was pretty happy about something and we wondered what it was. He seemed to have the same expression he had on his face when we had discussed the finer points of how we won the Cheryl Falcone lawsuit, sitting around my hotel room eating a delicious dinner in downtown Seattle, *and* how my testimony was what had made the most difference.

"I have two announcements," Paul began, with a small smile on his face. "First, we are going to begin a weekly hotel in-house newsletter. I will take suggestions for the name of the paper, and the winner will receive a crisp new $50 dollar bill, and dinner for two at Trader Vic's! Write your suggestions on a piece of paper, note the time and date, fold it, and hand them in to me, here. We will announce the winner at next week's meeting."

Immediately I grabbed a small notebook I carried with me, wrote my entry on a piece of note paper with the exact date and time, and passed it across the table to Paul. An extra fifty bucks would be great, and dinner at Trader Vic's was always a pleasure. I could take my mother, Clara, I thought randomly, to myself. Paul took the scrap of folded paper from me with a chuckle and a grin.

"The next agenda item is a happy one for us!" Paul said mysteriously. He paused and then added, "The Benson Hotel will be the site of the Western White House for a few days. We just received word that President Ronald Reagan will be staying here!" Paul was visibly excited, alternately pushing back his chair and standing up only to pace back and forth and then sit back down, again. Although many of the other department heads had experienced presidential visits previously, this would be Paul's first and he wanted everything to be, "just perfect for the president!" he said as he got up and continued his nervous pacing back and forth.

The year was 1984, in October as I recall, and I'd been on the job for almost five years, with so many things happening during that time. In 1980 I'd never have felt that the Benson was safe enough for the president, but after my improvements and safety upgrades, by 1984, I felt that the Benson *was* safe enough.

At the time, the election race and what President Reagan was up to in his reelection campaign was generally the most important news of the day.

I was nervous about all of this. I was the Director of Security. What would my role be? There were only three of us security employees on staff and we would need to be on our toes. We learned the *Secret Service Advanced Team* would be arriving the following day and we were to cooperate in any way, giving them unfettered access to anything they wanted. I would also be expected to explain the layout of the hotel, so they could provide the best security possible for the president. We would defer to them as *they* would be the ones in charge.

When I arrived at work the next day, looking extra sharp in the event I had to meet with any of the Secret Service, I found our grand hotel buzzing with employee activity. The "housekeeping men" were on ladders in the lobby removing each link of crystals from the elegant chandeliers, cleaning them with a sparkle solution, and wiring them back in place. Cleaning the crystals was a monumental task, as there are thousands of individual links on the many chandeliers in the grand lobby, but every detail had to be considered.

The lobby carpet was being cleaned, (the marble flooring was covered in beautiful burgundy carpet at that time) and there were teams of housemen cleaning the carpets in the guest corridors. Walls were being scrubbed with a mild cleaning solution, with all nooks and crannies dusted. The entire kitchen was steam cleaned by a work-crew that was kept overnight making sure the kitchen was sparkling clean by the time they were done.

I hate clichés but the kitchen was so clean you could eat off the floors!

Every president since president Taft had stayed at the Benson Hotel, at one time or another, and the rumor I heard was that Chef Bauser had served Presidents Eisenhower, Kennedy, Nixon and would now serve Reagan. I can't confirm that as fact, but it was a rumor I heard. Bauser's reputation for perfection was on the line, yet again. But I knew Chef Bauser was up to the task, because he was *always* up to the task. He was a brilliant chef, a real artist and completely dedicated to perfection.

The hum of activity generated an excitement, and that excitement spread like a virus. Every employee was infected with it, and their pride showed that the president of the United States would be staying — *at the Benson of course!* They smiled a little more, they talked among themselves and seemed genuinely happy to be part of the process of making everything at the hotel spic-n-span. It was a plum assignment, being able to prepare for the president's stay, and knowing the White House had chosen the Benson yet again.

This kind of assignment represented a kind of one-up-manship for the other Portland Hotels, who had never, and never would make the cut. This would include places like the Multnomah, the Marriott, and even our biggest rival — the beautiful Hilton Hotel.

The grand hotel would be spotless when the president and his men arrived and I was proud to be part of the goings-on, a little intimidated, I will admit, but damned excited, too. This would look good on my resume, I decided.

There was no way to prepare for the onslaught of *official-dom* coming our way, except to get out of the way, and do as the Secret Servicemen ordered. I was in my second floor office when Paul opened my door without knocking and ushered in a Secret Service agent. Paul never barged in without knocking first, except when it was important and he might be in a hurry. I stood up from behind my desk, caught slightly off guard and I could tell Paul was flustered, but happy.

"Don, this is Agent Bradshaw from the Secret Service Advance Team."

"Hello, I'm happy to meet you." I said.

I offered my hand as I came around my desk to meet him, and gave him a firm handshake. Bradshaw was about an inch taller than me, and had short cropped steel grey hair, barely longer than a military cut. His eyes were a very intense blue-green that swept over the room, and seemed to take in the entire area in one glance. Bradshaw had the command presence of an experienced lawman *or* soldier. His handshake was firm and his smile, bright but brief. It was strictly business with Agent Bradshaw. Both he and Paul sat in front of my desk in the two nice wing-back leather chairs I had wrangled from housekeeping storage just a couple of days before.

Bradshaw sat sideways in his chair keeping a good peripheral view of the office door. I could see the slight bulge of his sidearm beneath his dark gray suit jacket. It was time for business alright and the Secret Service was now in charge. "Happy to meet you Mr. DuPay. I'll be outlining our plan for security," he said, as if he was waiting for me to take notes. I sat down behind my desk and took out a large yellow pad and sat poised with my gold Cross pen waiting. Paul also took out his pen, and held it in his hand looking ready to jot something down if needed.

"Ok, you know we have a template for security at this hotel because Presidents' have stayed here previously," Bradshaw began. "Here's the deal. We will be taking over the entire seventh floor. All the rooms will be sanitized by bomb sniffing dogs and the rooms we're not using will be sealed off. The White House Communications Staff will be setting up all necessary communications the President requires. He has to be able to talk to anyone in the world by crypto communications. They will be placing antennas on the roof. The staff are all armed, of course."

"Yes, of course!" I replied pleasantly.

Bradshaw looked over at me, to make sure I was taking notes. Paul was paying close attention, shifting his pen from one hand to the other, but not writing anything down and looking a little overwhelmed. Agent Bradshaw looked at him skeptically, noticing he wasn't taking notes, in a disapproving way it seemed to me, but continued outlining the plan. I continued jotting down notes on the yellow pad that I thought were important, things I'd need to explain to my two security officers and everyone else when the time came.

"Communications staff will take up three adjoining rooms with their equipment, and will sleep in shifts in those three adjoining rooms. The President and first lady will be occupying the Crown Suite and it will be their personal living quarters while here. The Crown Suite will also be inspected, sealed, and guarded against entry until the President actually enters. The three elevators will be inspected by the elevator company employees and their equipment will be sniffed by our bomb dogs. Do you follow me so far?"

"Yes," I said, "perfectly!"

"One elevator will be for the exclusive use of the President and First Lady, and will be examined and sealed off before its use. The other two elevators will be rewired to prevent the elevator from stopping on the seventh floor. An agent will be in the elevator lobby 24-hours-a-day, just in case."

"Okay," I said.

Agent Bradshaw turned, getting more comfortable in his seat and again looked at Paul, questioningly, who looked back at him and smiled his most earnest smile, nodded his head ap-provingly, and murmured, "Yes, okay." I could tell Paul was liking the plan so far when he sat up a little straighter in his chair and continued smiling. It was clear he was enjoying the excitement and the importance of this new situation.

"All food for the seventh floor will be prepared by your chefs and inspected by the agents in the kitchen before being delivered. The agents will also watch while the chefs prepare the food for the seventh floor. A total of three agents will occupy the kitchen to observe the food preparation. One in the maintenance department, one supervising food prepared for the seventh floor and one agent examining all incoming groceries."

Bradshaw looked over at me as he explained, "We don't want a case of dynamite coming in with a case of frozen peas, you understand?" I nodded in agreement, understanding completely, and smiling at the comical image he'd just shared. So far they weren't missing a trick.

"As for the rest of the building," Bradshaw continued, "there will be snipers on the roof covering all four directions, as well as snipers on the roof of the US bank building on the east side of Broadway and atop the Western Union building at Broadway and Oak. We can land a helicopter on the roof if necessary for evacuation of the President as you already know from your own Fire emergency plans."

"Yes, I'm familiar with that," I said amiably.

"Good!"

Boy, these guys knew everything, if they *already* knew a helicopter could land on the roof. "And there's more than enough room for a chopper," I said, as Paul nodded his head in agreement.

"The fire escapes and Oak Street employee exit will also be guarded 24 hours a day," Bradshaw continued. "We will be making certain security up-grades to the Crown Suite. The bedroom where the President and First Lady will sleep will have bullet proof steel plates cut and installed in the windows so no one can shoot into the room. When the President and First Lady are sleeping, a military helicopter will be hovering overhead protecting the airspace. Fighter jets will be on stand-by while the President is in town. Concrete barricades will be placed blocking Oak Street, and SW Broadway will be barricaded except for one lane. This will prevent a truck bomber from crashing into the hotel building."

I continued taking notes, but Bradshaw was talking so fast I could barely keep up. This *was* important business, keeping our president safe.

"Now!" Bradshaw continued, looking over at us and giving us both direct eye contact to be sure we were attentive. "The President will be arriving from the airport in a protected motorcade. All overpasses going over the freeway on his route downtown will be patrolled by armed Portland police, with helicopter support overhead. The motorcade will arrive on SW Broadway and will use the underground parking entrance below the bank building at Broadway and Stark."

"Okay," I said.

"The President and First Lady will be escorted through the underground tunnel that runs from the parking garage, under Stark Street and into the Benson Hotel proper. They will be taken up to the seventh floor on their private elevator and made comfortable in the Crown Suite. That about covers most of the details of what will happen!" said Bradshaw in conclusion.

Turning to Paul he said: "Sir, if you have other business to attend to I can finish up here with Mr. DuPay." Paul, realizing he had been dismissed, stood up and assured us he did indeed have other business to attend to and backed out of the office, smiling.

"If you need anything, Agent Bradshaw, please just let me know," Paul said as he shut the door behind him. I had writer's cramp from taking notes and was glad to let go of the pen. I knew I had all the notes I would need. I was impressed with their plan and the high degree of professionalism it entailed. Bradshaw stood up and looked around the office and then sat down informally on the edge of my desk. "There's a lot more to talk about, DuPay," Bradshaw continued in a pleasant tone.

A couple of minutes later, room service knocked on the door with coffee and croissants. "Mr. Mannerly asked us to deliver this," said the waiter nervously. He walked into the room, and placed the silver tray and carafe on the opposite corner of my desk. The young waiter poured two cups of coffee, looking over at us hesitantly, and then backed out of the office, shutting the door quietly behind him. "We'd like your role here while the President is in town to be our liaison with hotel staff. How many security officers do you have?" Bradshaw asked as he picked up a cup of hot coffee.

"Two, a male and a female officer," I replied.

"We think they could be best put to use in the lobby and in front of the hotel while the President is here. I'm sure they know all the transients and other, you know, undesirables that may wander Broadway Street and they can do their part by keeping them out." I nodded my head resolutely.

"Absolutely, I'll inform them right away of their new duties."

"You need to understand that security will be very tight. The president and First Lady will be as secure *here* as they are in the White House. I know you must remember that President Reagan was shot back in March of 1981. I wasn't with them then, but nothing—absolutely nothing will happen to the President while *I'm* in charge here in Portland!"

"I understand."

Bradshaw had been looking around the room while talking but finally stood up and turned his intense blue-green eyes on me. "Not on *my* watch," he said again, looking me right in the eyes.

The *worst* thing that could happen is for the President to be killed here, I thought to myself.

"What do you think of when I mention the Ford Theater?" Bradshaw asked.

"That's where President Lincoln was assassinated," I answered coolly, knowing immediately what he was getting at.

"It was a wonderful theater for its time and produced many great plays, but it's not remembered for any of that. The Ford Theater is *where* Lincoln was shot!" Bradshaw raised his hand and slapped it down on the desk for emphasis. "The same thing would happen if Reagan was shot here. It would be the *only* thing the Benson Hotel would be remembered for." His short statement was intense, and the power of his professional presence brought home the gravity of the situation.

For a few fleeting moments, during the president's stay, the Benson Hotel would be the Western White House and the most important center and focus of the free world. I took a deep breath and let it out slowly, offering my hand to Agent Bradshaw and looked him right in the eyes. "We can handle it," I said calmly. "This *is* the Benson!" I said firmly in conclusion.

He smiled, nodded his head and gave my hand another firm shake. As he turned to leave, he said, "The bomb dogs will be arriving first thing in the morning to sanitize rooms," he said with a brief smile, glancing over his shoulder. "And it would be great if you could stay in the hotel while the President is here so we can have easy access to you, in case we need you for anything. That won't be a problem, will it?" he asked.

 "Not at all, I stay here often for inspection duties."

He nodded silently, as he walked out the door. As I watched the door close behind him, I sat back down in my chair, pushed back and stretched my legs, folding my hands behind my head, as I leaned back in the swivel chair. I had been a cop and detective for many years, and been involved in a lot of heavy shit, but this assignment topped them all it seemed.

Wow, the President was coming to town!

✶✶✶✶

It was a knock on my door that awakened me at 7:30 am the next morning. I looked out the peephole of my room. It was Agent Bradshaw. After letting him in, he got down to business, again.

"Good morning Mr. DuPay," he began. "May I call you Don?"

"Of course!" I answered, tossing my bathrobe on the bed, hopping into my suit pants and hustling into my dress shirt. He didn't seem to mind that I was dressing in his presence and I didn't either. We were two grown men and I *had* overslept a bit.

"Didn't expect you quite so early," I murmured, slightly embarrassed.

"Two teams of bomb dogs are waiting in the parking structure next door," he began.

"Alright," I said.

"We need to let them get to work."

I tied my tie, looking closely at my face in the mirror. I decided I could skip shaving until later, when I had time. As he stood waiting quietly, I walked into the bathroom, splashed my face with cold water, patted it dry with a hand towel, combed my hair and turned to face him.

"Your wife doesn't mind you spending a couple of nights in the hotel away from home?" Bradshaw asked.

"Sometimes I have to stay for the weekend, every few weeks. The department heads all have to do it. To inspect how things are going and make sure everything is up to snuff."

"I see."

"You make sure all the employees, waiters and cooks are doing their job right, so my wife understands. You know how it is. Besides, I like staying in the hotel. This mattress is better than my own and I get more pillows!" I chuckled, smiling at him.

"I definitely know how it is, having to be away from home," Bradshaw said.

"Yes," I murmured, remembering the two years I served in Germany, during the Cold War.

"I assumed you might stay on the eighth or ninth floor, overnight. Must be a better view from up higher, huh?" he asked distractedly, pulling aside the window curtain and looking down on Broadway street. I waited for him to continue.

"I was surprised when the Front Desk told me you were in 209 on the second floor."

"I always stay here in room 209. It's right next to the fire escape. Most people don't know anything about fire safety, *civilians*, you know? The fire department can't get a rescue ladder higher than the 5th floor. That's the main reason I stay in this room. It's much safer."

Agent Bradshaw turned and looked at me thoughtfully for a moment. I could tell he was wondering if he hadn't overlooked one important detail with this new information.

"Too bad the Crown Suite is on the 7th floor," I said, interrupting his thoughts. "But you guys could always take the President out a window and into your helicopter, in the event of a catastrophic fire but I don't think that's going to happen. I had all the rooms outfitted with smoke alarms a couple of years ago. When I was first hired, there wasn't a smoke alarm in the entire hotel. I changed that pretty quick."

Bradshaw nodded, mostly to himself, and smiled. "Well, the dogs are waiting," he said, opening the door and changing the subject. "They always are," I mumbled to myself, laughing. I hurried to catch up with him, as he walked ahead of me, straightening my tie on the run, one last time. The day had begun and the United States Secret Service was in town. We had things to do.

The two dog handlers were young military types dressed in black jumpsuits. They had short cropped hair covered by black baseball caps and black lace-up combat boots. They were superficially friendly when we were introduced, but their serious task was first on their minds and they were eager to get to work. Both dogs were beautiful black and brown German Shepherds, well-groomed and looked like they had just been bathed, with glossy coats and clean pink/brown paws. They sniffed my legs out of curiosity, dismissing me as a threat and then strained at their leashes eager to get on to sniffing something else.

Agent Bradshaw wanted to start at the bottom of the hotel and work up so the kitchen would be the first area inspected. Chef Bauser was cooking about a dozen large prime rib roasts for an evening banquet, and the heady aroma of savory meat filled the kitchen. The dogs sniffed and whimpered and pulled at their leashes. I thought having them in the kitchen was a little unfair. They were supposed to smell for explosives but all they could smell was prime rib, and they wanted some. Even the handlers were distracted. "It sure smells delicious in here," said one of the agents, pulling at a dog's leash.

One of the dogs stopped to sniff at Chef Bauser's pant leg as he was standing over a roast. Bauser ladled up the dripping juice, basted the meat and checked on the salted crust. The dog stopped and seemed interested in Bauser's wooden clogs. They were his regular work shoes and the wood had soaked up a great many kitchen spills over the years, becoming discolored and old looking.

Satisfied, the dog gave the chef a perfunctory final sniff and we moved to the bakery section of the kitchen. The baker was baking large sheets of wonderful rich, yellow, pound cake and smearing the finished loaves with creamy buttercream icing. The scent of the pound cake mixed with the aromas of the prime rib was almost too much for the dogs, who seemed nervous and distracted by all the fine cooking. I wondered if they had endured this level of distraction in their previous training.

"What's up with the wooden shoes?" asked Agent Bradshaw, motioning towards Bauser. I shrugged my shoulders, by way of explanation, saying: "Well, Bauser is Swiss, I think. They're his work shoes, he won't wear anything else, but we all get a kick out of it."

"We don't think his shoes are going to blow up or anything," Bradshaw said, breaking into the first grin I had seen on his face, "but we tend to check on things that are out of the ordinary," he continued philosophically. Bradshaw gestured around the kitchen at the other cooks busy at their tables.

"No one *else* is wearing wooden shoes," he said in a declarative way. Again I shrugged my shoulders. "They'd kill *my* feet," I said. "But you can hear Bauser coming when he clip-clops around. We've gotten used to them. It's part of his culture, you know. He's not from around here." Agent Bradshaw nodded his head, "Oh, I see" he said, chuckling.

Finishing the kitchen inspection, we were off to inspect the elevators. I grabbed a tasty sliver of prime rib from the edge of one of the slicing tables, and popped it in my mouth, nonchalantly, savoring how delicious it was. One of the cook's spotted my blatant theft and shot me a disapproving glance but said nothing. After all, what could he say to such a high personage as myself, on such a lofty mission? I was, after all, working with the Secret Service to make sure our president was safe during his sojourn in Portland.

I tried to keep out of the way as the elevator company employees jumped into the pits at the bottom of the old Otis Elevator shaft, inspecting the greasy tracks of long cables. Each elevator was raised and lowered manually, by way of a lever, so they could control the speed. It moved in slow motion and each cable was inspected for damage or wear, while the dogs waited, bored, sniffing and whining. They found nothing exciting in the inspection of the elevators and whined to get on to the next thing. The elevator the president would use was then sealed until his arrival, after it had been secured and then approved as safe.

Next, we took the newly "sanitized" elevators up to the seventh floor, Agent Bradshaw, two Portland police officers in jump-suits, two German Shepherds, and myself. The dogs continued to sniff, whine and squirm. There was no further conversation, only the mild awkwardness of being in a crowded elevator with strangers.

The doors opened and the two dogs jumped forward leading the parade. I handed Agent Bradshaw a master key, attached to a keychain, sporting a sterling silver Tiger ornament. The key would unlock all the rooms on the seventh floor. Once the rooms were approved by the bomb dogs the seventh floor would be off limits to all but the Secret Service men. I followed along as each room was opened and inspected, staying out of the way of the dogs and nodding to hotel staff, (in my cheerful attempt to look more official than usual) and staying out of the way of the Secret Service men, who were trying to do their jobs.

The last room to be examined was the lovely Crown Suite. Only brand new pink bed linen was used to make the king sized can-opied bed the President and First Lady would be using. New pillows, and a beautiful shaded gold and green satin bed cover-let hung elegantly to the floor. It looked as if it had been made from a tapestry belonging to a French king and was extremely ornate, with embroidery and embellished ribbons. I learned it had been ordered especially for the President and first lady, and was of course brand new. I looked out the bedroom win-dows down onto Oak Street seven floors below and then over at the buildings across the street.

These were the windows that would be blocked by steel plates so the President could sleep safely without risk of sniper or bomb attack. I could visualize a helicopter levitating in midair 500 feet above the Benson. I caught Agent Bradshaw's eyes searching the room. He was taking in every detail and the stress was showing in his face by the set of his clenched jaw and the squint of his eyes.

There is only one President of the United States and it was Bradshaw's job, at that time, along with many other men, to keep our president alive and well.

The following morning my job was to assist the White House Communications Staff in bringing their equipment up to the seventh floor. I commandeered the room service elevator and watched as a dozen or so large wooden crates were off-loaded and wheeled into the rooms that would handle all White House communications. They allowed me to watch for a few minutes as they un-crated their equipment. Boxes were pried open and the devices inside set to work immediately. It was obvious they'd done this many times before. Their motions were practiced, with an easy military precision that I couldn't help but admire.

Within thirty minutes the male operators were talking on phones, and checking the manuals for proper frequencies. When they noticed me still standing there, looking into the room, one of the men smiled, walked over and closed the door in my face. I had been politely excused. My services were no longer needed. It reminded me a little of my days as a uniformed cop and how often I had said these words to a gathering crowd: "Move along, now. There's nothing more to see here. Move along. Move along, now." I didn't take having the door closed in my face personally. It was just business.

With nothing more to do except look important in my suit, I took the elevator down and stood on the mezzanine over-looking the lobby and watched the hum of a hardworking staff getting ready for something important. I watched Norma, my security person with her arm on the shoulder of Laurie. She was slowly turning the beggar lady around and escorting her back out the Oak Street door. Laurie was mumbling something to Norma, probably something like, "I can't even sneak in here anymore," but I'm just guessing on that, as Laurie's entreaties were imaginative and endless, and always sounded sincere.

As Norma turned her head and looked up, she saw me and caught my eye. I waved, gave her the thumbs up and smiled ap-provingly. She was doing her job, watching for those troubled "unwanteds" with all their drama, noise, and unpleasant smells, and she was keeping them at bay.

Watching the comings and goings reminded me when I was a kid one summer. Because I'd been so curious, I removed the back from an old clock to see all the wheels, springs and gears moving together to accomplish one purpose, to move the hands on the face. The staff at the Benson was like a well-oiled clock and it was a pleasure to behold. Frankly, I was proud of the place *and* my role as Director of Security.

Later that evening, Agent Bradshaw issued me a "basement pass," that would allow me access to the lower level elevator lobby. I would be one of the privileged few to see President Reagan and Nancy Reagan arrive at the Benson, and then pass through the underground tunnel from the secure parking fa-cility under the bank across Stark Street. After we had assembled, the chosen few observers stood quietly looking at each other awaiting the first view. I could almost hear the song playing in my head: *Hail To The Chief.*

After only a few moments of waiting, the President and First Lady finally appeared, preceded by three Secret Service agents in front of them and three more in back. They walked in a protected cocoon of very serious looking armed men. The President made brief but deliberate eye contact with each of us, and smiling, he turned and disappeared into the elevator. That was it! The only time I was able to see him coming or going was that single instant and it lasted less than 30 seconds.

Now, the Benson was really buzzing. The President and First Lady were in the building and occupying the Crown Suite! Though it was almost a hushed feeling, the ripple of excitement was just below the surface, but it was everywhere. The feeling in the hotel was electric. The staff was hyper aware of these most important personages, and the bellmen and housemen walked with a more business-like step, standing tall.

Added to this excitement was the now constant surveillance of the staff by the Secret Service. Chef Bauser prepared the evening meal for the Crown Suite, moving from side to side in his wooden shoes under the watchful eye of an agent, occasionally smiling nervously at the agent but saying nothing.

Another agent supervised the groceries being received by the kitchen staff even before Bauser could look at the invoice. The employee entrance was watched and every employee was checked for a proper ID badge which had been signed by me, before being allowed to enter the hotel. There were snipers on the roof, and agents gazed expressionlessly at anyone exiting the hotel near any of the fire escapes, which were closely monitored at all times.

One agent monitored the lobby looking down from the mezzanine, another sat in the lobby pretending to read a newspaper. The seventh floor was off limits to all, and only employees with access badges were allowed to deliver food or linens and were supervised by agents while doing so.

Looking in from the outside things would appear normal, but the Benson Hotel was now an armed camp. Each of the Secret Service agents carried an Uzi, 9mm machine gun under their suit jackets. The Uzi is about 24 inches long in total with a 10 inch barrel and can fire 600 rounds per minute. The President was protected by a virtual platoon of machine-gun-carrying men in dark blue suits. This was impressive and made the hair on the back of my neck stand up at times.

God help anyone who tried to harm President Reagan while staying at the Benson Hotel.

Agent Bradshaw had done a superb job of spinning a virtually unassailable steel cocoon around the leader of the free world. As darkness settled over Portland, the President of the United States was sleeping in luxury in the Crown Suite and I was in room 209 on the second floor, too excited to do anything but look out my second floor window and think about it all.

Below me, parked on Broadway was a Fire Department hook and ladder truck stationed there for the duration. I could see the flashing lights of the police car manning the concrete barricade limiting Broadway Street traffic to only one lane. Red traffic cones dotted the street as lane indicators. Traffic was kept as far away from the front of the hotel as was practical.

As I stuck my neck out the window, I could hear the chop-chop humming and buzzing of the helicopter as it hovered overhead for several hours, nonstop. I felt safe with a fire truck below me, and a Secret Service agent with an Uzi just a few feet away, standing inside the fire escape stairwell, along with a police-man on the street corner.

Opening the window all the way I could feel a slight breeze, just enough to flutter the curtains. I walked over to the bed and lay down. I was surrounded by a pile of feather pillows in pink pillowcases, and as I drifted off to sleep, I fantasized all this security was for *me*. I fell asleep thinking *Air Force One* was waiting for me at the airport and ready to take me back to DC as the leader of the free world.

Instead, I woke up at about three a.m. disappointed I was no longer the President, but just in time to watch a second heli-copter arrive on station, to relieve the first one. It must be refu-eling time I surmised, as I watched the chopper's red running lights winking off into the distance as it flew across a slate grey sky. Returning to bed I fell into a comfortable sleep.

Day two of the President's visit began early. The entourage was up and out of the hotel by nine sharp. Though President Rea-gan was gone for the day, making speeches, shaking hands, and posing for photo opportunities, there was no relaxing for the remaining Secret Service guarding the hotel, and no let-up on the constant surveillance of the staff.

Maids and housemen seemed extra glad to get off work, scurrying down the street towards home. It was difficult for them being constantly monitored and watched as they made up beds, vacuumed corridors and removed room service trays, by Secret Service men, armed with Uzi machine guns. The kitchen staff was the *most* watched and some of the cooks seemed to perspire more than usual in the hot kitchen environment. By comparison, having Chef Bauser look over the kitchen staff's shoulders was nothing like being watched by Secret Service agents with bulky Uzi's barely concealed beneath their suit jackets.

Although Agent Bradshaw was vague about the arrival and departure times of the Presidential Party, the hotel grapevine always seemed to know. "The President will be arriving back in a few minutes," whispered Jim Gimarelli, our concierge, glancing at his watch. He covered the corner of his mouth with his hand, as if he were telling me a secret in jest, while he sat, leaning forward at his lobby desk. I smiled, passed by on the way to my office, and nodded as if I already knew.

It was six in the evening and I decided to have dinner brought to my room by the room service waiter. It was the same waiter who had been cleared to bring food to the Crown Suite. He also gave me a knowing smile and whispered: "The President will be retiring at nine P.M. I've been excused for the night after nine, and I'm the *only* one allowed in the Crown Suite!"

He took a deep breath and unconsciously puffed up, smiling to himself, as a way to show me how important he felt to be the "only one" allowed in the president's suite. Again I smiled as if I already knew, and said, "This is kinda fun, huh?" He smiled back and nodded and I waved him a casual goodbye and began munching my sandwich and salad. It was a good piece of prime rib with horseradish sauce left over from the day before. One good thing about working at the Benson was the kitchen leftovers were always stellar. Whatever *was* left over, prime rib, cheese cake, perfectly made salad, it all went to the employees, and we sure did enjoy it.

After I finished my sandwich I peered out my room window down at the street, below. Flashing lights from the Presidential Motorcade were moving slowly up Broadway, first the motorcycle cops, then the President's limousine, with red lights flashing, and more cops following. They disappeared into the parking garage, safe from public view. I thought about trying to see the president one more time by waiting in the lower elevator lobby for the party to appear through the underground tunnel, but decided against it. I had no further duties except to be in the hotel just in case Agent Bradshaw needed me for any reason.

So, I laid down on the comfortable bed and fell asleep with my clothes on. I was awakened by the startling whop-whop-whopping of the helicopter arriving on station. I got out of bed, looked out the window and glanced at my watch. It was after nine and dark outside. The president was safe in the Crown Suite. Once again, I went back to sleep, feeling I could finally relax.

At seven the next morning the room service waiter knocked on the door and brought in my coffee and croissants. "The President's gone now," he said. "We're allowed access to the seventh floor, again." It was the same waiter who had delivered my prime rib sandwich the night before, and he still had the same pleased knowing look. "We can get back to normal now," he added as an afterthought. Then he wiped his brow with an imaginary handkerchief, and we both laughed quietly, as I nodded in agreement, repeating, "back to normal, yes."

In five minutes I ate two perfect butter croissants, gulped down my coffee and arrived on the seventh floor just in time to see the last box of the communications equipment going down on the room service elevator. It would then be loaded onto a waiting rental truck parked on Broadway in front of the hotel.

Yes, President Reagan and First Lady Nancy were gone. I could almost feel the hotel breathe a collective sigh of relief. It was like the four main walls of the building inhaled the fresh air and then exhaled in unison. We were back to normal again. The genuine stress of being *Benson-Hotel-perfect-for-the-leader-of-the-free-world* was thankfully gone.

I never saw Agent Bradshaw again, or President Reagan. They didn't stop in to say goodbye, but they did leave several boxes of book matches in various parts of the hotel. Emblazoned on the cover was the Presidential crest and the name *Ronald Wilson Reagan*. I kept one as a souvenir. But I was also left with an admiration for the professionalism and absolute tunnel vision focus of the US Secret Service in keeping our president safe. I hoped they paid Agent Bradshaw well. I couldn't imagine having to perform his duties and deal with the huge level of stress that was heaped on him because of it, on such a regular basis.

Announcing the Winner

A few weeks later, the naming of the Benson Hotel in-house newsletter that Paul decided we needed was announced. After President Reagan left Portland, the next department head meeting, a few days later, became a critique on our overall performance during the president's stay.

On the day of the meeting, with all of the department heads seated around, Paul stood behind his chair at the head of the conference table. He was pacing a little as if he were gathering his thoughts. He stopped pacing for a moment and put his hands on the back of his chair, getting ready to speak. Instead, he just smiled at us, as if he enjoyed our discomfort, making us wait. We sat forward in our chairs expectantly, wondering if we had somehow messed up and were about to get chewed out, but no, Paul was still smiling. This was theater, and Paul was enjoying his moment.

"I want you all to know," he began, choosing his words carefully, "how proud I feel today as the manager of the Benson Hotel. Your performance in your everyday duties during the president's stay was exemplary. I have been assured by the White House staff that you made their visit most comfortable." He looked at each of the department heads including me, as he continued praising our performance. In the back of my mind, I hoped he would remember his words when it came time for me to ask for a raise.

Finally, Paul slowly, deliberately, removed his wallet from his breast pocket and opened it. Thumbing through it, purposefully taking his time, he brought out a crisp new $50 dollar bill and held it in his hand looking at each of us in turn.

"This is the $50 dollar prize money for naming the new hotel newsletter."

He looked at each of us, as we all sat forward expectantly. He waited a moment, then said: "It goes to our Security Director Don DuPay!" Of course it would be me and winning the little contest didn't surprise me, though I *was* pleased.

There could be only *one* name for the newsletter and that was *Simon Says!* And that was my entry. There were a few "aw shucks!" groans from two other department heads who had written the exact same entry, but mine was the first written down, dated and timed and handed into Paul all those weeks before in front of everyone.

I stood up and reached across the table and accepted the cash and then stood waiting for my two dinner tickets to Trader Vics. Again, Paul thumbed through another part of his wallet, slowly extracting the tickets, continuing the suspense. With the tickets in my hand and the fifty in cash I made an expansive gesture of my own, befitting the bit of theater Paul had provided, and took a deep bow.

"Thank you! Thank you very much!" I said playfully, trying to mimic Elvis. Everyone laughed at my good imitation of Elvis and began to get up to stretch and go about their day. I took my own sweet time putting the cash and tickets into my wallet. It was my moment. And I enjoyed it as much as Paul had.

When the Band JOURNEY Came to the Benson

During my last year at the Benson, we had a bit of drama when in 1986, the rock band *Journey* came to Portland and booked rooms at the Benson. Like many rock bands that stayed at the Benson, they were known as rabble-rousers. I had a dim view of bands coming to the Benson because they routinely trashed the rooms. I tried unsuccessfully to get Paul to agree not to do business with them, but he refused. Their money was good, he said and if there *was* any damage, the hotel was always generously compensated later.

However, even after all my safety and security upgrades, I still had to deal with people trying to bust into the kitchen. The band *Journey* proved no different and one memorable night, it got out of hand.

It was well after midnight and I was working in my second floor office finishing up paperwork for Paul. Each call or interaction between guests and security or ne'er-do-well "unwanteds" as they were called was documented with a file number and a written report. We generally had two to three per day and documenting their hijinks and identities was a tedious but necessary part of the job. It often reminded me of when I'd been a street cop, writing those endless reports at the end of shift.

As I sat at my desk, filling out forms, I noticed that "Laurie" had been seen begging in the lobby again. Just then the ringing of my telephone interrupted my thinking. It was the night phone operator informing me that the janitor in the basement kitchen was being harassed by some very drunk and possibly "high" hotel guests. When I asked who they might be, and how many, I was told they were from the rock band JOURNEY and that there were *six* of them. I had watched them swagger into the hotel earlier the previous day and was aware of their presence, but didn't know who they were, other than some rock band I'd never heard of before.

The Benson had been through this before with rock bands, and I had suggested for years that we refuse to serve them because of how badly they behaved, trashing the rooms and having loud parties with young girls in attendance, many of whom were underage. We had grown tired of the antics of these men, and the stories that circulated in the hotel industry were well-known, even if they didn't hit the newspapers. It seemed hotels from all over the country had a sad tale to tell regarding some wild group of drunk rock musicians who didn't know how to act like adults.

As I stood up from my desk, I cranked up my official *Director of Security* aura and prepared for battle. I buttoned up my three-piece suit jacket, locked my office behind me and took the elevator down to the basement.

Once I exited the elevator, and walked into the kitchen, I heard yelling and cussing. When I walked into the kitchen, I found six male band members from the band. I could see that the band members were upset that they couldn't get into the locked kitchen cupboards and the coolers. They were guests of the hotel, but they were milling about and trying to raid the kitchen, behaving like a bunch of kids having a sleepover at a friend's house when their parents were out of town.

"We're lookin' fer sumthin tuh eat!" one of the men said defi-
antly.

"We wanna make sum samiches!"

"You can't do that. You'll have to go somewhere else, the kitchen
is closed for the night."

"Aww, come on, we're hungry!"

I told the group of men, who appeared to be in their 30s, that I
was the security director and they were trespassing and had to
either go back to their rooms or leave the hotel. I had been ad-
dressing the larger group of men, but there were another two
to the side of me that I couldn't see. The janitor stood nearby,
cowering and looking worried.

The next thing I knew I was lying on the floor, on my side, having landed on my left arm.

One of the men, without warning, sucker punched me on the
jaw which completely knocked me down. As I lay there, the
wind knocked out of me, I felt immediate pain in my upper left
arm. I moved my shoulder but the rest of my left arm couldn't
move and I began to groan in pain, cursing now under my
breath. It was as if from the elbow down my left arm was par-
alyzed.

After they saw I was injured, they scrambled away like rats
abandoning a sinking ship, *and* like the sneaky cowards they
were.

The janitor helped me up and guided me to a chair, rushing
over to a telephone to call for help. A few minutes later, the

Night Office Manager also showed up (after being alerted by the phone operator) of the assault, and rushed downstairs to help.

My memory is sketchy after that point because I was in so much pain but I do remember being loaded into an ambulance and the hurried, bumpy ride to the hospital. After several x-rays and some needed pain medication, the ER doctor put me in a huge cast, *after* surgery that is! I was in a cast from my waist to my neck, with my left arm bent at the elbow, and sticking forward of my body as if I might be preparing to shake hands with someone.

To say the cast was cumbersome and uncomfortable would be putting it mildly!

I was also furious that I'd been assaulted and injured so seriously, but after talking with Paul, he begged me not to make a big deal out of it. In other words, he asked me *not* to sue the band, as any kind of lawsuit would be made public record. If the incident became part of the public record, the media could write about how the rock band Journey came to the Benson Hotel and assaulted the Director of Security. It would be *bad* press for the Benson.

But there would be a workers compensation settlement, Paul promised me.

Later x-rays would show, the bone in my upper left arm had been shattered in three places, and recovery would be long. I remained at home for a few days getting used to my plaster prison and ruminating. I would be like this for FIVE months, I was told by the doctor!

Five months?!

And five months it was, and it changed all aspects of my daily life. Sleeping was hard, using the bathroom was hard, having relations with my wife became a challenge. Eating became more difficult, getting in and out of the car became difficult.

Everything became more difficult.

The doctor also told me that *if* the damaged nerves ever grew back, it would take "months to years for that to happen," and my left arm would, "never be the same." Because nerve damage is serious and complicated in a man fifty-years-old or older, the doctor told me. And he was right.

My upper left arm has never been the same since the 1986 assault!

In winter, when it gets particularly cold, my upper arm aches and bothers me, and I have occasional nerve pain that travels down the length of my arm, and the back of my hand and the backs of all five of my fingers. I have literally taken *thousands* of aspirin over the years in an effort to deal with the regular discomfort and pain.

Shortly after the assault, I talked with my wife and we agreed that if I remained away from the hotel for five full months, my job might be gone when I returned. I would have to keep working. She altered my suit jacket so I could wear it with my arm sticking forward of my body, which meant I could continue to come to work every day wearing a suit. It worked. I looked ridiculous, but it worked nonetheless.

I met with my security officers several days after the assault and explained things would be different for a while. They would have to pick up the slack and *my* job would be mainly administrative. Whereas I'd always been able to do my rounds, and be a hands-on type of engaged boss, now I'd need to take it easy, so I could heal. They all understood and were more concerned that I get better than any change in our regular routine.

A week after the assault, I showed up at work encased in my huge plaster cast, with my arm poking out like a deranged dictator. I was back working, and I was *still* the boss of security. Paul knew I was hot about what happened, and I reminded him on more than one occasion of my disdain for rock bands for the very reason that they were habitually immature men with no regard for other people. They partied, snorted coke with local minor girls they would pick up after shows, and routinely trashed hotel rooms, even going so far as to bust up windows and mirrors. They had no regard for the personal property of other people and behaved like animals.

Despite my disgust at what happened, and my reasoning behind not wanting to do business with rock bands, I was unsuccessful in mandating the future exclusion of any of the well-known rock bands from the Benson. The hotel, Paul said, was not in a position to turn good business away. After agreeing not to call a lawyer and make a stink, which *would* have gone public, I received a 10% disability settlement from workers compensation.

My final compensation? A check for a whopping *two* thousand dollars!

Some of my law enforcement friends were furious at the tiny check, and told me I should sue and try to get more money, and though I could have, it would have meant going public, leaving the job and causing embarrassment for the Benson Hotel.

I couldn't do it.

****

The Benson Hotel never had a company picnic. Somehow, picnics seemed too blue collar for such a highbrow place like the Benson, but they held company banquets at different fine restaurants in and around Portland. After the presidential visit, our banquet was to be held at the Thunderbird Motel and Riverside Restaurant. The Thunderbird, at that time, overlooked the Willamette river near the East side Coliseum sports arena. Though no real competition to the upscale Benson Hotel, the Thunderbird was known for fine dining, and was a suitable location for the Benson's annual company banquet.

We were all excited as we met at the Thunderbird that night, gathering together to form a small group. The round dining tables seated eight. Each table had white linen tablecloths that hung nearly to the floor. Cloth napkins folded to look like little tents were placed over the silver service.

Each Benson department held sway at one or more tables. Chef Bauser sat surrounded by most of his assistant chefs. And Freddie, the Catering Manager had a corner table, with a few of her own staff seated with her. The head table would be seating Paul, Janet, the Purchasing Agent, myself, and the *comptroller*, a petite woman named Bonnie, with a degree in accounting, a sharp pencil, and reading glasses on her nose. She seemed to be counting plates and tables, and writing things down. She would be the one paying for this shindig, but with company money of course.

At our table, I sat with Jim Gimerelli, and Marty from PBX, as well as Gayle Patman, the Front Office Manager. She was sitting next to Victor, my security man giggling and holding hands with him under the table. A romance had blossomed between Gayle and Victor. I suspected something was up when I saw Victor hanging around the front desk when Gayle was working and smiled to myself when Victor's change of address form crossed my desk a few weeks later. He had moved in with her. Good for both of them, I remember thinking. Gayle had a changed look about her. She was happy and relaxed. Whatever they had going on, I decided it was a good thing. Maybe Gayle wouldn't be an old spinster after all.

Marty was talking about retirement. She told us that her "last year" was coming soon. She looked tired and bent over, as if she was always permanently humped over the PBX board. I would miss her. We had become friends and I knew I could trust her. She was discreet and kind, always letting me know she cared about me, asking about my health, did I feel okay, did I need anything, a cup of fresh coffee, or a bowl of hot beef vegetable soup.

Looking around the room, I saw all the folks I worked with in a new setting, in their street clothes and relaxed with a drink in front of them. It was the first time I had seen Chef Bauser without his two foot tall Chef's hat on. He had hair afterall! I thought I could see a permanent indentation on his forehead where the Chef's hat always rested, but figured it might just be my imagination.

Next to Chef Bauser was Sou Chef Jimmy Hufana. Jimmy was romancing a pretty blond that worked for Freddie in Catering named Cindy. They made an interesting couple, hiding in the background at first probably because they were different races and worried what people would think. They too seemed happy and I was happy *for* them.

A few stragglers wandered into the banquet area, among them Charlotte the cocktail waitress. She looked over the remaining available seats and decided it would be okay to sit at the same table with security. She picked a seat next to Norma, who was looking content with herself. Norma's matronly, motherly, school teacher persona worked well for her as a Benson Hotel security officer, and as she saw Charlotte sit down, they began to chat easily, smiling and laughing. Charlotte was perfectly made up, of course, coiffed and perfumed as well. She looked beautiful and she knew it. I wondered what she looked like when she was by herself at home, or if she woke up looking perfect like that.

Cocktails began at six, with dinner served at six thirty. I ordered a glass of red Sokol Blosser, as it was the wine usually served at the Benson and I had grown to like it. I swished it around in the glass sniffing it like I knew what I was doing, and held up the glass to toast around the table. "Here's to us!" I said. "Yes, here's to us!" several people echoed.

I never did figure out the wine thing, but pretended I had, acting like I knew just how to appreciate the scent, body and subtle flavors of wine, when in reality I knew *nothing* about wine, only that I enjoyed drinking it.

The table conversation was casual, small talk about President Reagan's visit, nudges and smirks over the love affairs going on right in front of us. We had survived a presidential visit, a tough assignment for any staff, and had come through it on top of the world. There was a renewed camaraderie among us. Looking around the room, it seemed like we had all become family.

But six thirty came quickly, about two glasses of wine for most of us, and still Paul hadn't arrived. We began to look at each other, slightly concerned, and almost as if we were asking each other permission to begin eating. We waited a little longer, but hungry now, we began nibbling at the salad the staff had placed before us. I had chosen a shrimp cocktail on a bed of lettuce, with Bleu cheese dressing on the side, and after a couple of mouthfuls we all but forgot about Paul showing up.

That is until I noticed Marty, who had a view of the entryway, had suddenly stopped chewing. A piece of lettuce hung forlornly from the corner of her mouth, and her eyes were opened wide. We all took a cue from Marty and looked in the direction of the entryway to see a man dressed in a black wetsuit, complete with goggles and flippers looking every bit like the creature from the Black Lagoon.

"Who could *that* be?" I heard someone say.

As this man lumbered into the room and approached the table, he removed his goggles. We were astonished to see the man was soaking wet and dripping water on the floor. He laid his speargun aside and pushed his wet hair off his forehead.

"Hey guys! Sorry I'm late," he said. "I thought I'd do some fish-ing on my swim over!" We all just about dropped our forks when we realized the man standing and dripping in front of us was none other than Paul Mannerly!

We didn't know how to react. Had Paul lost his mind? Was this a joke? Was this macho beast from the dirty Willamette River really the mild mannered, often tentative Paul Mannerly? Had he really put on a wetsuit, to swim across the Willamette River, then crawl up the adjacent riverbank and just walk in the front door of the Thunderbird?

We were floored.

For a long and awkward moment, we all just stared at this apparition, dressed in black, dripping water. He stared back at us unsure of himself, a hopeful smile on his face.

Finally, Bonnie, the bookkeeper started laughing, and then applauding, slowly at first and then with more vigor. Then, everyone else took up the clapping and it escalated to a few whoops and whistles from the Chef's table. The proverbial ice had been broken. Paul smiled broadly and without removing his flippers, clopped to his place at the banquet table. This was the grand entrance of *all time* and would be the first short article of the first ever printed *Simon Says Newsletter,* as I noticed someone in the group had begun taking photos of Paul with a small camera.

The servers came with our entrées, and the meal was of course, impeccable. The Thunderbird staff knew they were serving the famous Chef Bauser and the crew of the Benson. We had salmon or chicken, with wild rice, and steamed vegetables, in an herbed butter sauce.

I watched and listened as some of the Thunderbird staff whispered about the guy in the frogman's suit. They had never seen anything like it either, and I had to chuckle. Paul sure had made a grand entrance at the dinner, but it really added to the fun!

After we were all thoroughly stuffed, we stood around laughing, shaking hands and saying goodnight, and then went our separate ways. We were full and happy and proud of ourselves for so many reasons. I walked the three short blocks to my car and drove home. It was nice to be home and comfortable in my own bed, with only the ticking of my old windup alarm clock, and my sleeping wife beside me.

Epilogue

The stories you have just read are true. The people were real and the incidents depicted actually occurred. All the known characters existed and all the details are as true to my memory as is possible to document on paper. It is my remembrance and my perspective of working at the Benson Hotel as it operated decades ago, recorded to the best of my recollection.

When I joined the staff, I found this elegant landmark hotel dangerously encumbered with outdated business practices that no longer served the safety of the rich and famous clientele the Benson catered to on a daily basis. There was not *one* smoke detector anywhere in the entire building, no evacuation plan or *Emergency Response Team* in the event of any unforeseen troubles, crimes or fire events.

Key control was something none of the managers even knew was a term, let alone understood how it worked. The Keys to any given room had been proliferated and reproduced so many times no one on staff knew how many keys had been cut for any particular room *"over the years"* and were still floating around in Portland.

I was able to make many changes in policy and operating procedures that made the Benson not only one of the most elegant addresses in Portland but also the safe hotel that it needed to be, for the important clientele it served. In doing so, I gained the respect, over time, of most of the hotel staff members and I had a lot of fun leading in that capacity. Being the Director of Security of the Benson Hotel was certainly one of the best jobs I ever had, after leaving the Portland Police Bureau where I worked for over 17 long and demanding years.

The memories I have of that time in my life, helping to usher the Benson into the 21st century remain a cherished part of who I am to this day.

Today, the Benson Hotel is *still* the most elegant and respected hotel in Portland Oregon, but things *have* changed. A proliferation of new and upgraded hotels in the downtown area have seriously increased competition, and the resulting loss of revenue as well as some (in my opinion) unfortunate management decisions have dimmed the glint on the carving knife.

The decision to divest itself of the famous Trader Vic's restaurant was clearly a mistake of management. The well-known Trader Vic's has been replaced with a steak house they call El Gaucho. A nice place for certain, but essentially no different than any other good Portland steak house such as The Country Kitchen or The Ringside on Burnside Street.

There are many such steakhouses in Portland but there was only *one* Trader Vic's, and to go there, you had to go to the Benson.

The elegant London Grill, the Benson's other great restaurant, is also essentially now closed, too. It is available only for special occasions and planned events. A lack of revenue was cited as the cause for that change. However, despite these sad changes at the Benson, the same wonderful food is still served in the lobby lounge, now renamed The Palm Court.

I remained on staff at the Benson until late 1986 when Westin Hotels, the management company, sold out to a foreign firm. I elected to leave at that time and do private consulting work for hotel management companies instead, often testifying in court on various lawsuits as an expert witness on hotel security. I felt I had done enough to help ensure the general safety and continued safe operation and success of the Benson Hotel.

I made many important changes and it was simply time to move on. I came to this decision because under the new management, we would be replaced one by one anyway, and we all knew it and I would likely have been the first to go on that proverbial chopping block. The sense of family that we had enjoyed would ultimately be destroyed and so I decided my time at the Benson had run its course.

Before leaving, in my off time, I spent my last year with the Benson selling copies of a pamphlet I had written and published the year before on hotel management. It was called *The Delicate Balance: Risk Management for Hotels,* which I sold for $10.95 cents per copy. It was full of common sense information on how to keep guests and employees safe, and what constituted "reasonable care" in hotel management.

The corporate office in Seattle was not pleased with everything I claimed in the little book, according to what Paul told me, but that was okay. They could have their opinion, but I was the one with the background in law enforcement, and I felt these were things I simply had a better understanding and grasp of due to my career as a police detective.

In 1986, the Benson Hotel was also placed on the *National Register of Historic Places,* which would protect the hotel from the possibility of demolition.

Needed improvements continued when in 1990 a 17 million dollar renovation was required to upgrade many parts of the hotel that needed restoration and repair. This meant the Benson would continue with its reputation as the finest hotel in Portland, and retain their many dedicated longterm customers.

Looking back now, I am so grateful, upon reflection, that I was able to work at the Benson Hotel, for the time I was there. Because with my determined advocacy *and* my policy changes, I helped make the old building a much safer place for all concerned, for both guests and employees, including the ever grumpy but *brilliant* Chef Xavier Bauser.

If you are ever looking for a great place to stay overnight, in a comfortable and elegant hotel, with friendly and gracious staff, or perhaps you merely want a sumptuous 5-star meal, prepared by some of the city's finest chef's, I would encourage you to visit… the Benson of course!

In early 2023 the Benson Hotel completed a "multimillion dollar upgrade" which includes new lighting, wall coverings and new furniture by the Dutch furniture design company, Moooi. Other upgrades include new flat screen televisions and a state-of-the-art WIFI system, for internet service for all the rooms.

Afterword

Simon Benson would live to be 90 before passing away August 5, 1942. He became a dedicated philanthropist in his later life, and one of Portland's most notable citizens. In the early teens, Benson donated $100,000 to the Portland School District to assist in the building of a school. Six full city blocks at NE 12th and Hoyt were purchased and the project was begun. The school was designed by architect Floyd Naramore, (1879-1970). The Benson Polytechnic opened September 4, 1917 and has educated thousands of young Portlanders over the intervening decades.

Simon Benson was also responsible for making Multnomah Falls the beautiful park that it is today. He helped spearhead construction of what we now call the Historic Columbia River Highway, which goes from Vista House to the falls and beyond. Multnomah Falls was already a favorite attraction; people could visit by train or steamboat. Benson knew it should be the centerpiece of the highway, so he bought the falls and hundreds of surrounding acres, then donated it to the city of Portland as a park, ensuring that it would not be turned into a tacky tourist attraction. The city of Portland later gave it to the US Forest Service.

Simon Benson left his mark upon our city, and the Benson Hotel is still the finest hotel in town!

The Benson Hotel in the 1900s. Photo courtesy of Scott Allen Tice.

Simon's Place

Acknowledgements

I would like to thank all the people I worked with at the Benson Hotel for their humor, generosity and support. The unexpected happenings that occurred there become funnier as the years pass and I see how lucky I was to help make the Benson Hotel a safe, fun place for Portlanders and out of towners to visit. My advocacy and important policy changes seemed mundane at the time, but looking back I see how important they were.

I would like to thank the people I worked with, who have been mentioned in this book either by their full names or only by their first names. Their friendship and camaraderie was very important and I remember them with affection and good humor.

I'd like to thank my wife, Theresa Griffin Kennedy, editor of this and many other writing projects for her tenacious editing and hardwon knowledge of the publishing industry. Theresa is a dedicated writer, author, editor and publisher and I recognize her important role in my books being introduced to the world.

Theresa would not take no for an answer when I told her I didn't think anyone would care about my time working at the Benson Hotel. I'm glad I took her advice when I began writing these stories. My wife has good writerly instincts and she knew my stories would be entertaining, informative, and good Portland history. Theresa makes me a better writer and I thank her for everything she does to make my books a reality, including this, my fourth book. I would further like to thank my beloved late Mother-in-law, Doris Anna Griffin, for acting as a beta reader and proofreader for this project. As a "nit picking" grammar aware person, Doris made important suggestions for how to polish the manuscript and make it better and my wife Theresa, her daughter, incorporated *all* of those wonderful suggestions.

Additionally, I would like to thank *Scott Allen Tice*, a popular Portland photographer, for generously helping with the images used in this book. Your help made using those images possible, Scott, which made the book that much better!

And I would like to thank Fred Leeson, Bruce Haney, Robert Crane, JB Fisher, Sean Davis and Suzy Vitello for their wonderful blurbs!

I would also like to thank Chester Benson, and Sig Unander, the great grandsons of Simon Benson, for their help in correcting vital information regarding their grandfather's history, his name and other family logistics.

~ Don DuPay

About the Author

Don DuPay was born in Wenatchee, Washington where he spent most of his childhood, later moving to rural Montana for a short time living on his parents farm. He settled in Portland, Oregon permanently in 1947 at the age of eleven. DuPay graduated from Grant High School in 1954 and later studied for 2 years at Lewis and Clark College. He went on to spend 3 years active service duty in the US Navy performing top-secret radio surveillance on the Baltic Sea, during the Cold War. He rose to the rank of Cryptographic Technician T-branch E-6. From there, DuPay joined the Portland Police Bureau in 1961. In 1967, at the age of 31 he rose to the rank of detective and was later promoted to homicide detective. DuPay worked for PPB until 1978 when he resigned for documented medical reasons. He became the director of security for the Benson Hotel for several years in the 1980s, and was instrumental in changing hotel safety policies that would ensure better safety for customers and manage fire code violations. Later DuPay volunteered as co-host of a cable access television program called Cannabis Common Sense, with host Paul Stanford. In 2017, DuPay graduated from Portland State University. He was honored in the commencement program for being "the oldest" graduate of that year. DuPay resides in Portland with his 4th wife, author, poet and editor, Theresa Griffin Kennedy. *Simon's Place: Stories from the Benson Hotel* is his fourth book.

About the Editor

Theresa Griffin Kennedy was born in Baker, Oregon and has lived in Portland, Oregon since she was eight-months-old. She is a writer of creative nonfiction, poetry, literary fiction in the genre of domestic noir, and crime history. She works as a freelance editor and is the publisher and editor of Oregon Greystone Press. In 2013 Kennedy completed a masters degree in Adult Education, Leadership and Policy, and in 2014, a masters certificate in Teaching Adult Learners. Kennedy is an advocate for prison reform through education, literacy and creative writing. She has been published in literary reviews, magazines, newspapers, several anthologies and in online news sources. Kennedy is the author of six books, including *Blue Reverie in Smoke: Collected Poems 2001-2016*, *Burnside Field Lizard and Selected Stories*, *Talionic Night in Portland: A Love Story*, *Beyond Where the Buses Run: Stories, and The Lost Restaurants of Portland, Oregon*. Kennedy is hard at work on her second novel, *The Angry Garbageman of Thurman Street*. She is a native of Portland, Oregon, and is married to Don DuPay, a writer, author, and a retired homicide detective who worked with PPB from 1961-1978.

References

DuPay, Don. (2015). *Behind the Badge in River City: A Portland Police Memoir*. Oregon Greystone Press.

Kennedy, T. G. (2022). *Lost Restaurants of Portland, Oregon*. The History Press.